JOYFUL & SPIRITUAL

Recipes for Body and Soul

Julia Reno & Sofia Kauko-Valli

JOYFUL & SPIRITUAL

Publisher Information

America Publishers
Email: info@americapublishers.com
Publisher & Creative Director: Lark Wells
Copy Editor: Albert Torres
Art Director: Julia Reno
Layout Design: Tom Hendricks
Digital Design & Production: Josh Edwards
Proofreader: Zayne Herbert

ISBN Information

eBook: 979-8-9925800-2-0
Paperback: 979-8-9925800-0-6
Hardcover: 979-8-9925800-1-3

For information about special discounts for bulk purchases, please contact Julia & Sofia.
Special Sales at: mgmt_jr@yahoo.com or wellnesswave@gmail.com

Printed in the United States of America

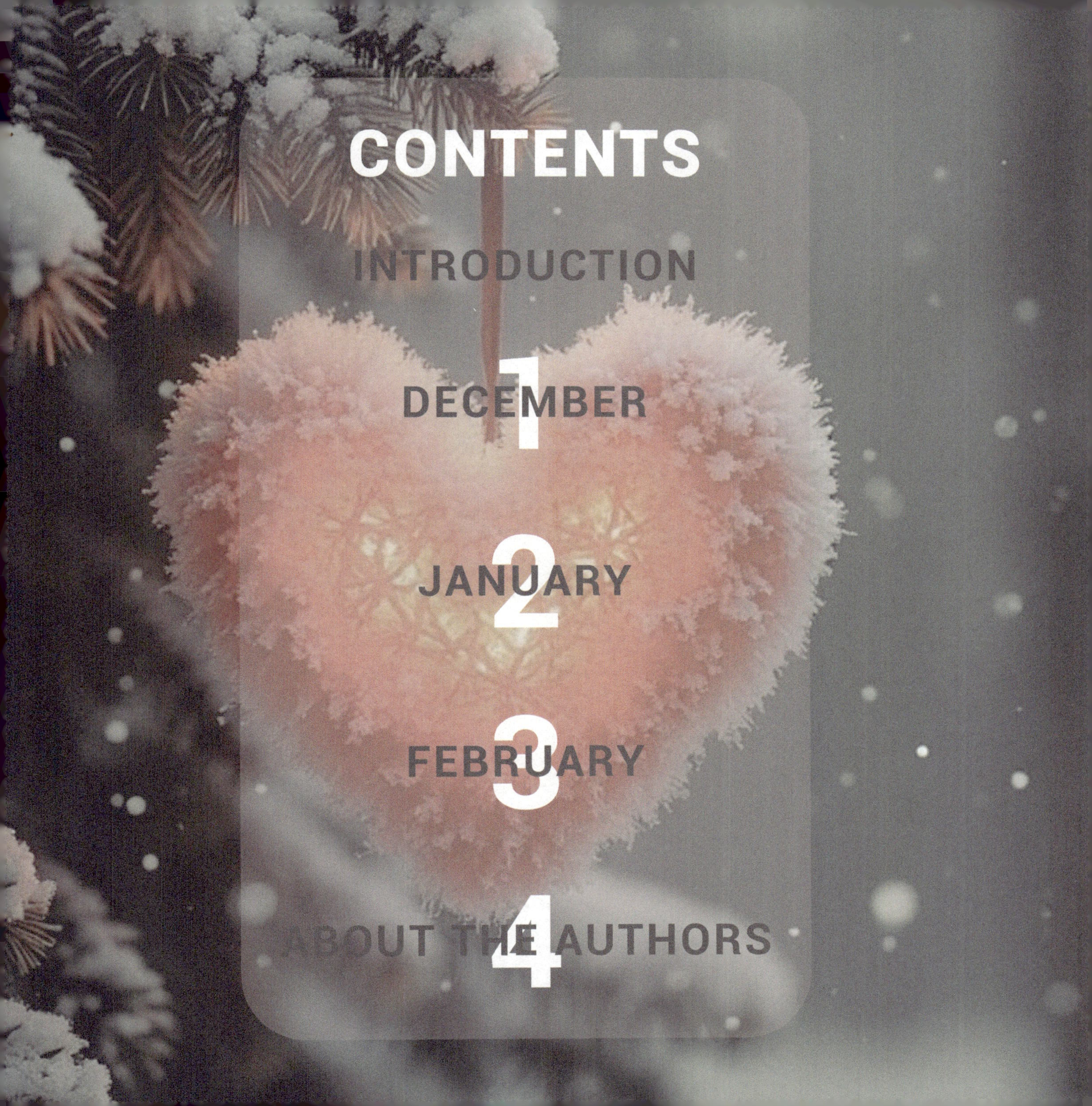

CONTENTS

INTRODUCTION

1 DECEMBER

2 JANUARY

3 FEBRUARY

4 ABOUT THE AUTHORS

I love summer. I am definitely a summer girl. Summer always makes me super happy. The sun is shining, birds are singing, and I can roam about barefoot. Our beautiful lakeside cottage is cozy and inviting, and I can not stop marveling at the beauty of nature in full bloom. There is always something fun to do. Swimming in the lake or just enjoying a refreshing cup of coffee on the patio.

The autumn is pretty OK too. Colorful leaves and getting back into the city mode are always thrilling. Maybe a new school year starts, new students are arriving, and there is excitement in the air. And then? The dreaded winter. It is cold and dark and wet everywhere until the snow comes. Then it is just cold and dark. Forever. My mood sinks at the mere thought of it.

This year, I am deliberately taking a different approach to winter. I am going to fully embrace it. And use it as a time of refreshment and contemplation, getting inspired again. This book is an invitation to all of us who want to get closer to God and find inspiration in His Word. It is time to enjoy the season to the fullest with family and friends.

Let's find refreshed faith and inspiration together!

Sofia

INTRODUCTION

This book stands as a testament to my gratitude and devotion, a reminder of how God's presence infuses every part of my being. I am not perfect, but dedicated to learning and growing through Jesus's teachings. He is the ONLY perfect person who ever walked the earth. I am endlessly thankful for his examples, sacrifice, grace, and mercy, and I seek to honor him in all that I do.

Also, this book is dedicated to my family and friends. Each one of you has inspired me and played a role in shaping my life in one way or another. I view all of you as valuable assets to learn from, and despite the outcome of our relationships, they make me who I am today - stronger, more purpose-driven, and more experienced. I am grateful for every single one of you.

My special thanks to my beloved family who pray with me, for bringing me food and coffee to keep me going on my sleepless nights, and believing in me. There are not enough words to describe my love and gratitude for all your support. Thank you!

Now, sit back, take a deep breath, and enjoy this journey with us over the course of the winter season. I am confident that this book will bring you peace and comfort.

Love you forevermore!

Julia

INTRODUCTION

DECEMBER

CHAPTER 1

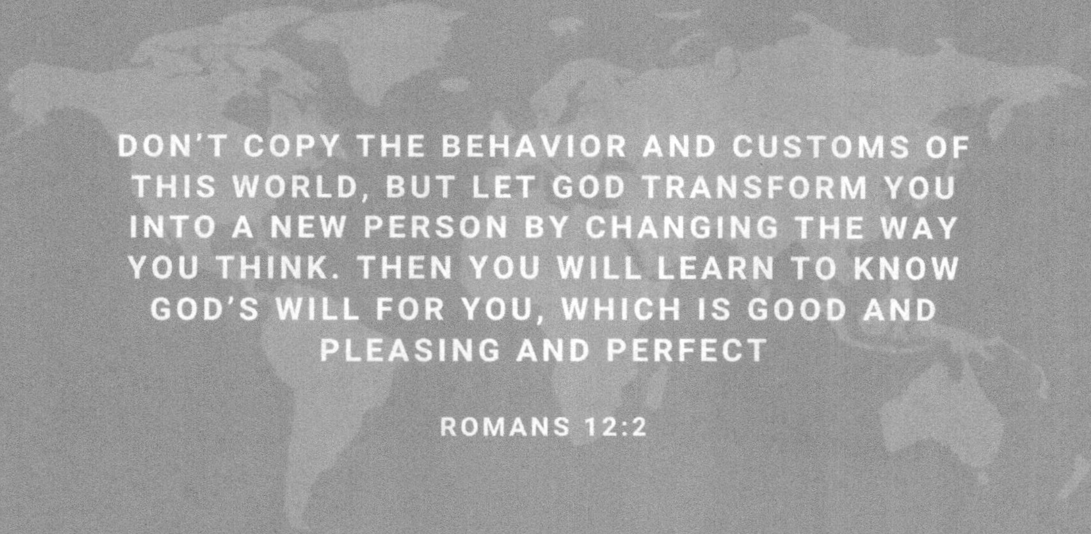

DON'T COPY THE BEHAVIOR AND CUSTOMS OF THIS WORLD, BUT LET GOD TRANSFORM YOU INTO A NEW PERSON BY CHANGING THE WAY YOU THINK. THEN YOU WILL LEARN TO KNOW GOD'S WILL FOR YOU, WHICH IS GOOD AND PLEASING AND PERFECT

ROMANS 12:2

UNITED STATES FINLAND

“
BEHOLD, HOW GOOD AND PLEASANT IT IS WHEN BROTHERS DWELL IN UNITY!
PSALMS 133:1

Despite the unknown road ahead, a faithful friend named Sofia Kauko stood by my side. Yes, you saw her name on the cover. Together, we started a challenging journey to write this book, pouring our hearts and souls into every word and facing obstacles and doubts along the way.

During this time, we've shared our personal struggles and challenges, along with our faith in God and our passion for sharing our life journey to inspire others.

One day, feeling particularly worn out, I found myself lost in a whirlwind of uncertainty. I began to doubt whether the project would come to fruition this year amid the chaos of my overwhelming schedule. It felt as though the dream we shared was slipping further and further out of reach.

But just when hope seemed faint, an unexpected package arrived in the mailbox. I opened it to reveal the most precious gift of a friendship - "belief in us" in the form of the first printed version of our book. Tears of gratitude and joy filled my eyes as I held the first book of our shared dreams and hard work.

FRIENDSHIP IS
THE SWEETEST GIFT

The words of a familiar Bible verse, Ecclesiastes 4:9-12, echoed in my mind: "Two are better than one because they have a good return for their labor. If either of them falls down, one can help the other up. But pity anyone who falls and has no one to help them up."

I whispered a prayer of thanks for the gift of my friend Sofia. She has been a pillar of strength and support in my weakest moments. Deep in my heart, I knew that this unexpected blessing was not just a reminder of the importance of having someone by your side through every trial and triumph. It was a testament to the power of friendship, faith, and perseverance. Thank you, Sofia!

Julia

PLUM CAKE

THE RECIPE YIELDS 6 SERVINGS

INGREDIENTS:

- 1/4 CUP BUTTER, SOFTENED
- 6 LARGE EGGS
- 2 CUPS ALL-PURPOSE FLOUR
- 2 CUPS SUGAR
- 3 TEASPOONS GROUND CINNAMON
- 3/4 TEASPOON BAKING SODA
- 1/2 CUP VINEGAR
- 4 CUPS DICED PLUMS (OR APPLES)

DIRECTIONS

STEP 1

GATHER INGREDIENTS. PREHEAT THE OVEN TO 350 DEGREES F (175 DEGREES C). LIGHTLY GREASE AND FLOUR A 9X13-INCH BAKING PAN.

STEP 2

BEAT EGGS AND SUGAR TOGETHER IN A LARGE BOWL WITH AN ELECTRIC MIXER UNTIL FOAMY.

STEP 3

ADD FLOUR AND CINNAMON. MIX UNTIL WELL COMBINED. ADD DICED FRUIT. STIR IN GENTLY PREMIXED BAKING SODA WITH VINEGAR AND THE REMAINING INGREDIENTS.

STEP 4

POUR BATTER INTO THE PREPARED PAN. BAKE IN THE PREHEATED OVEN UNTIL A TOOTHPICK INSERTED INTO THE CENTER OF THE CAKE COMES OUT CLEAN, 25 TO 30 MINUTES. COOL IN THE PAN FOR 10 MINUTES.

STEP 5

SERVE WITH A SPOONFUL OF VANILLA ICE CREAM. ENJOY!

“
OUR FAITH WILL BE LIKE GOLD THAT HAS BEEN TESTED IN A FIRE
1 PETER 1:7

Have you ever watched a fire and compared it to faith? Take a seat and look at it. They both can be powerful forces in different ways. Fire is often associated with destruction and chaos, capable of causing harm and devastation if not controlled or contained. On the other hand, faith is usually linked to belief, trust, and hope, providing comfort and guidance in challenging times.

In some contexts, fire can also symbolize purification and renewal, much like how faith can inspire transformation and growth in individuals. Both fire and faith have the potential to ignite passion and drive within people, leading to positive outcomes in various aspects of life.

The comparison between faith being like gold tested in a fire and life's challenges being like a fire is a metaphor often used to convey the idea that going through difficult times can strengthen one's faith and character.

Just as gold is refined and purified when subjected to intense heat in a fire, our faith can also become stronger and more resilient when it is tested by life's challenges. The struggles and obstacles we face can serve as opportunities for growth, self-discovery, and developing a deeper sense of trust and reliance on our beliefs.

We've read, heard, and watched movies about families who faced challenges in their relationships. Families that grew distant over the years due to misunderstandings and disagreements.

WHAT IF IT IS YOU?

But what if it's you? What should you do?

Every story is two-sided or even more. I personally went through challenges in the past several times. Just to name a few: abuse, lies, and cheating. Sound familiar? It's because every one of us has to be tested by God. The Bible says that God tests people by allowing them to face situations where they must choose between right and wrong.

These tests are meant to strengthen and purify people's hearts and to help them grow into strong disciples who live by faith.

In the midst of those dark periods, I turned to my faith in God for solace and guidance. I prayed, seeking clarity and understanding amidst the pain and confusion. I knew that God had His purpose for these trials and that He would carry me through.

I prayed for strength to overcome those challenges, wisdom to accept things I could not change, peace for my soul, and love the way He does. Forgiveness came slowly along with the healing of wounds.

"
BUT AS GOD TESTED AND APPROVED US BEFORE ENTRUSTING US WITH HIS GOOD NEWS, SO IN WHAT WE SAY, WE ARE SEEKING NOT TO PLEASE MEN BUT TO PLEASE GOD, WHO TESTS AND APPROVES OUR MOTIVES
1 THESSALONIANS 2:4

While the scars of the past remain, I'm still able to walk confidently in the grace and love of Jesus Christ, knowing that he has overcome all things for me. I know that God had a plan for me, and today, as I continue to put my trust in Him, my new relationships are better than ever, and my heart is filled with joy, trust, and love.

And so, my story became a testament to the power of God's love and grace, a reminder that even in the darkest of times, there is always hope for a brighter tomorrow. 1 Thessalonians 2:4: "But as God tested and approved us before entrusting us with His Good News, so in what we say we are seeking not to please men but to please God, who tests and approves our motives."

Today, I'm grateful for my trials and tribulations because they transformed me into who I am today, much like how gold is transformed into a precious and valuable metal through the refining process. It gives hope that our faith, when tested and proven genuine through adversity, can shine brighter and more precious, ultimately making us stronger and more steadfast individuals.

Ultimately, while fire and faith may seem different on the surface, they both possess an inherent intensity that can shape experiences and influence outcomes. Enjoy watching a fire.

Julia

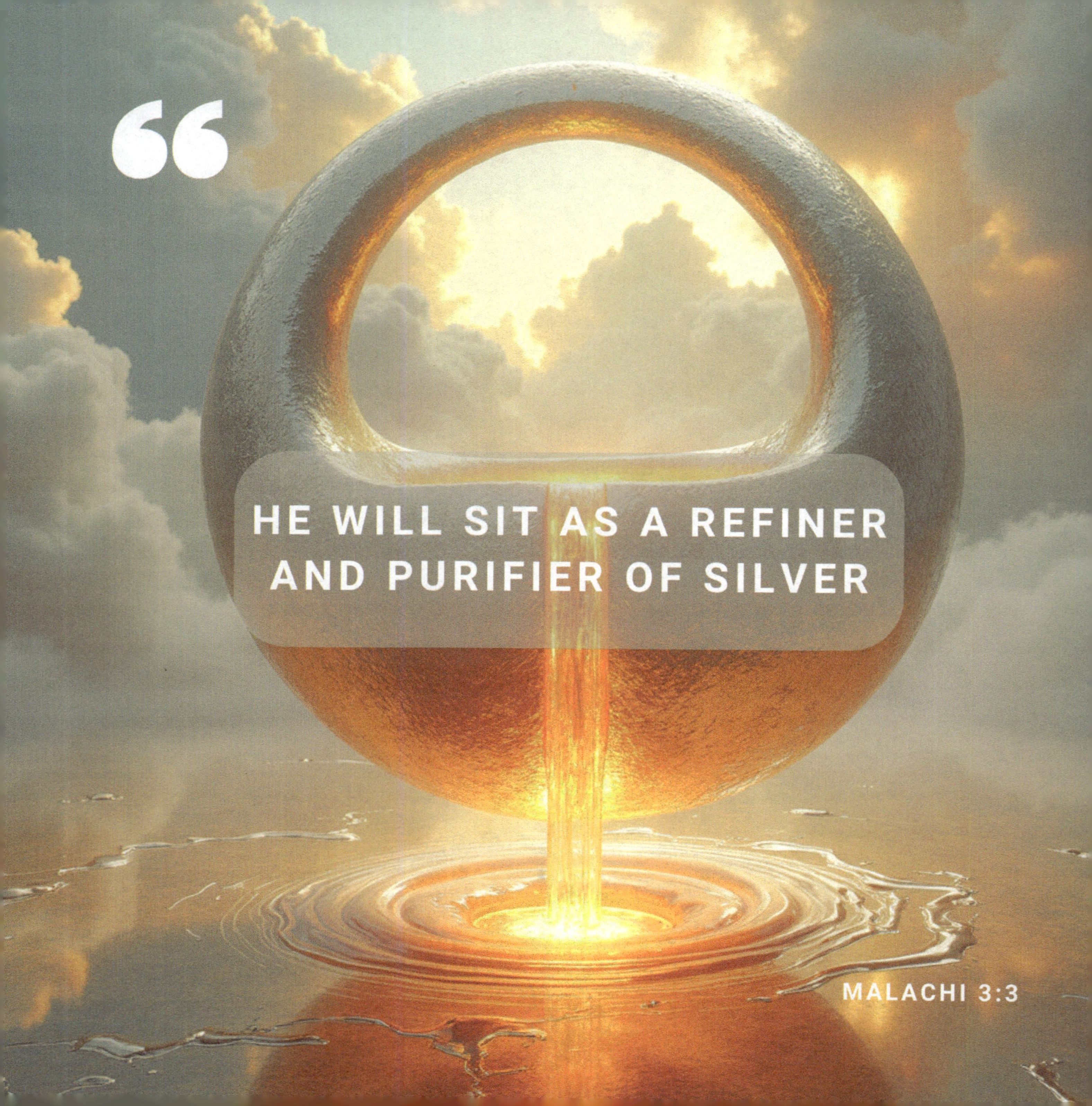
“
HE WILL SIT AS A REFINER AND PURIFIER OF SILVER
MALACHI 3:3

Did you know?

Sometimes, when we are going through a time of testing, we are tempted to think that we are all alone, even deserted. We may be prone to believe that life happens to us instead of happening all for us. We feel lonely and isolated. Nothing could be further from the truth. God is always for us, and He is close to us at all times. Some even say that He is the very breath in our lungs - we are in Him. That is close and intimate.

Do you know how silver and gold are purified?

It takes intense heat. I am sure you know that. But the precious metal is not left in a fire on its own. For the purifying process to be successful, the silversmith has to keep a keen eye on the melting silver, never leaving it out of sight. He has to stay close and actually watch the silver the whole time!

The intense heat burns away all impurities. Do you know how the silver smith knows that the silver is finally pure? Because he can start to see his own reflection on the surface of the newly melted silver. This is how God is purifying us. We are not alone. He is with us every step of the way until we start to reflect on Him and His qualities in our lives. I think this is so comforting to know when we go through hard and challenging times. He is close by, watching and taking care of everything. He will not slumber. Although the process may feel super painful at times, I am sure it is all worth it - we get to reflect God in our lives. What an honor that is! Let his love intimately embrace you today, wherever you are. You are loved!

Sofia

BE CREATIVE

THE BEST FLU SHOT

WINTER CAN BE TOUGH FOR SO MANY REASONS, BUT ONE OF THE BIG ONES IS HOW OFTEN WE FIND OURSELVES BATTLING COLDS AND THE FLU. IF YOU'VE EVER FELT LIKE THOSE SNIFFLES SNEAK UP ON YOU, THIS REMEDY IS HERE TO HELP! IT'S A VERSATILE, NATURAL MIXTURE DESIGNED TO SHORTEN FLU SEASON—OR EVEN HELP YOU AVOID IT ALTOGETHER.

MY KIDS USED TO JOKE THAT THE SECRET TO ITS EFFECTIVENESS IS HOW IT KEEPS PEOPLE AT A DISTANCE—BUT TRUST ME, IT'S WORTH IT! PACKED WITH IMMUNE-BOOSTING INGREDIENTS, THIS MIXTURE WILL HAVE YOU FEELING BETTER IN NO TIME. THIS IS ONE OF THOSE RECIPES THAT KIND OF GROW ON YOU OVER TIME.

HERE'S WHAT YOU'LL NEED:

- 1 CUP ORGANIC HONEY
- 1 TABLESPOON CAYENNE PEPPER
- A FEW GARLIC CLOVES
- GRATED FRESH GINGER
- 1/2 TSP GROUND TELLICHERRY BLACK PEPPER

PREPARE A SMALL GLASS CONTAINER TO STORE THE MIXTURE IN, AND THEN POUR IN THE HONEY. ADD CAYENNE PEPPER, THINLY SLICED/MINCED GARLIC, GRATED GINGER, AND FRESHLY GROUND BLACK PEPPER. MIX GENTLY AND REFRIGERATE. THIS CAN BE USED AS IS: TAKE A TEASPOONFUL WHENEVER YOU FEEL FLU SYMPTOMS SNEAKING UP. MAKE A SHOT: 1 TSP OF THE MIXTURE IN SOME LUKEWARM WATER. TEA - 1 TSP MIXED WITH HERBAL TEA. I HAVE EVEN TRIED IT ON TOAST AND MADE SPICED BUTTER FOR A STEAK WITH IT! BE CREATIVE!!

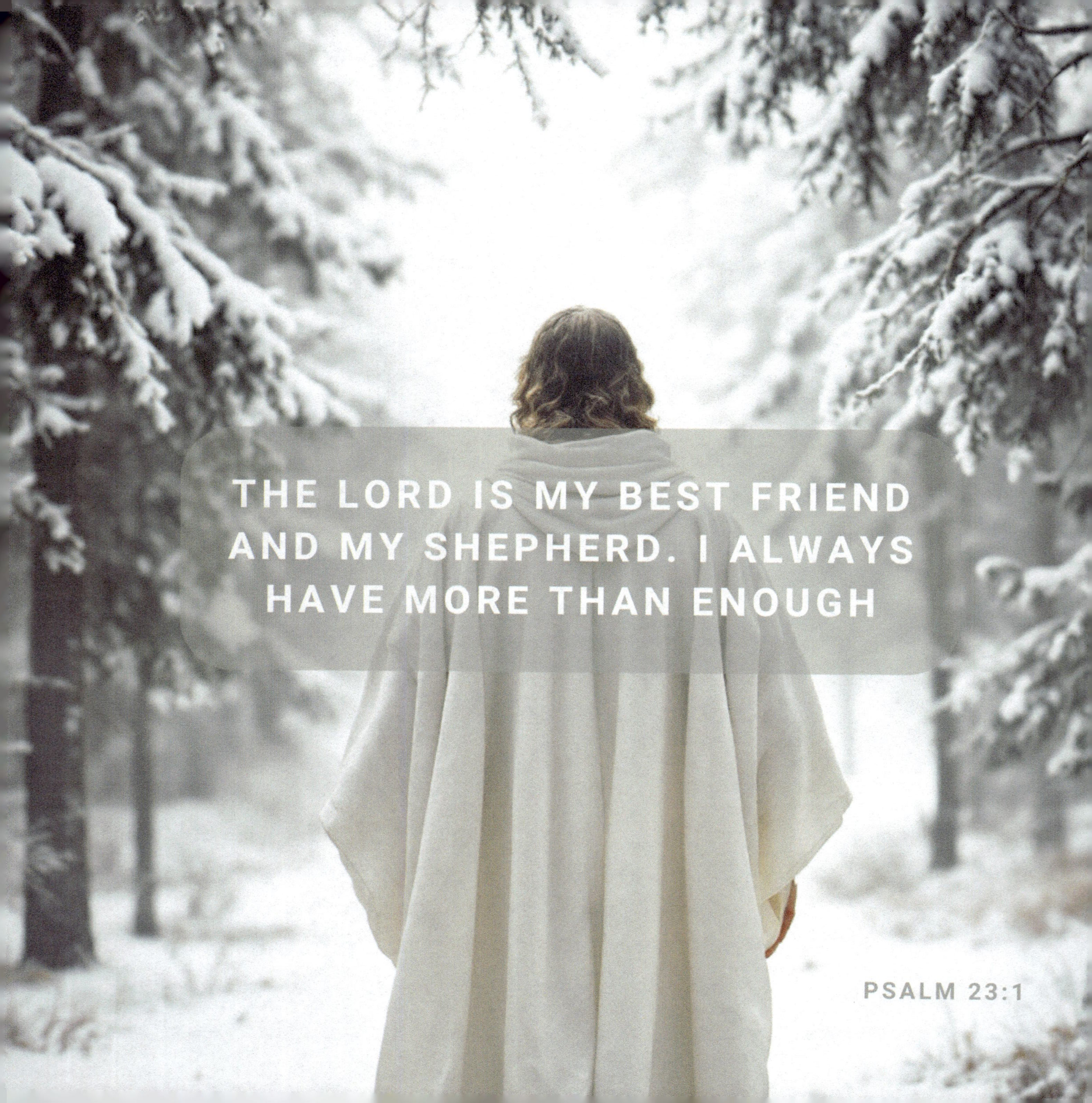
THE LORD IS MY BEST FRIEND
AND MY SHEPHERD. I ALWAYS
HAVE MORE THAN ENOUGH
PSALM 23:1

“The Lord is my best friend and my shepherd. I always have more than enough.” Psalm 23:1

This is one of my favorite scriptures in the Bible because it reveals how Jesus is everything to us. He is our best friend, and at the same time, He is the one leading us, ensuring we don’t lose our way. When you pause to reflect on that, it’s truly amazing. How comforting and reassuring it is to know that He is always there for us—rain or shine!

One day, during my quiet time with God, I felt inspired to study more about sheep. What an eye-opener it was to learn about them! Although sheep are clever and can express complex emotions like us, they are also prone to wandering and getting into trouble on their own. They need daily guidance and abundant care from their shepherd. Sheep are easily confused and lost. Yet, what’s truly wonderful about sheep is their relationship with the shepherd. I discovered that they have a deeply trusting bond with him. They recognize the shepherd’s face and voice and are eager to spend time with him.

Today, this verse speaks to me about the fearless and abundant life we have in Christ. No matter the season, we are never alone. He wants to remain our faithful friend through every stage of life, and His friendship offers us unending abundance. Because He loves us and tenderly cares for us, we can always approach Him fearlessly—with joy and happy anticipation—just as we would any dear friend. We are truly seen and deeply loved!

HE KNOWS WHAT WE NEED

Sometimes, entering the winter season can feel challenging. The darkness and biting cold can be overwhelming—even depressing at times. Where I live, the winter season is particularly long, with heavy snow and seemingly endless darkness. I often find myself feeling frustrated and tired. But guess what? God knows. He sees every part of our journey—the highs and the lows—and He isn't surprised by the shifts in our moods or energy. In His infinite wisdom, He knows exactly how to care for us in each moment. The truth is, there is a perfect purpose for every season.

I've come to realize that there's incredible wisdom in the rhythm of the seasons. Just as the world around us changes, we are invited to change as well. Winter, in particular, seems to call for something very specific: a slowing down, a savoring. And while slowing down may feel counterintuitive—especially in a culture that prizes constant busyness—it can also be profoundly transformative. Winter offers us the perfect opportunity to pause and embrace the gift of rest. It's not about laziness or stagnation; it's about giving yourself permission to breathe, reflect, and simply be. These are the moments where clarity often comes, where we can listen more closely to His voice, and where we can reconnect with our deepest selves. Winter may seem barren on the surface, but beneath the frost, preparation is happening. Just as seeds lie dormant beneath the snow, waiting for spring, so too can we use this time to cultivate what God has already planted in our hearts.

Let us ask Jesus to lead us to embrace the wisdom of seasons and create a wonderful and joyful time in Him.

Sofia

DON'T STRESS
ABOUT ANYTHING

SWEET POTATO SOUP

WHEN IT IS COLD AND DARK OUTSIDE, THE THOUGHT OF THIS HEARTY SOUP MAKES ME SUPER HAPPY. IT IS EASY TO MAKE, AND YOU DON´T HAVE TO STRESS ABOUT ANYTHING. MANY DIFFERENT COMBINATIONS OF VEGETABLES WORK FINE HERE, AND YOU CAN USE HERBS, TOO IF YOU LIKE. THE SECRET LIES IN ROASTING THE VEGETABLES SLIGHTLY.

YOU WILL NEED:

- 3 MEDIUM SWEET POTATOES
- 2 CARROTS
- 1 MEDIUM YELLOW ONION
- A FEW GARLIC CLOVES
- FRESH GINGER
- 3-4 CUPS OF VEGETABLE BROTH
- 1 CAN FULL-FAT COCONUT MILK / CREAM
- 2 TABLESPOONS OLIVE OIL / BUTTER
- FRESHLY GROUND BLACK PEPPER, SALT
- FRESH HERBS (CORIANDER, BASIL, PARSLEY)
- SOUR CREAM, OLIVE OIL, AND CASHEW NUTS FOR GARNISH

PLACE THE PEELED AND CHOPPED SWEET POTATOES, CARROTS, ONIONS, AND GARLIC ON AN OVEN-PROOF DISH AND SPRINKLE WITH OLIVE OIL, SALT, AND GROUND PEPPER. ROAST GENTLY ON MEDIUM HEAT UNTIL THEY GET SOME COLOR. HEAT THE VEGETABLE BROTH AND MOVE THE VEGETABLES INTO IT UNTIL FULLY COOKED. ADD COCONUT MILK AND PUREE THE SOUP. GARNISH AND ENJOY!

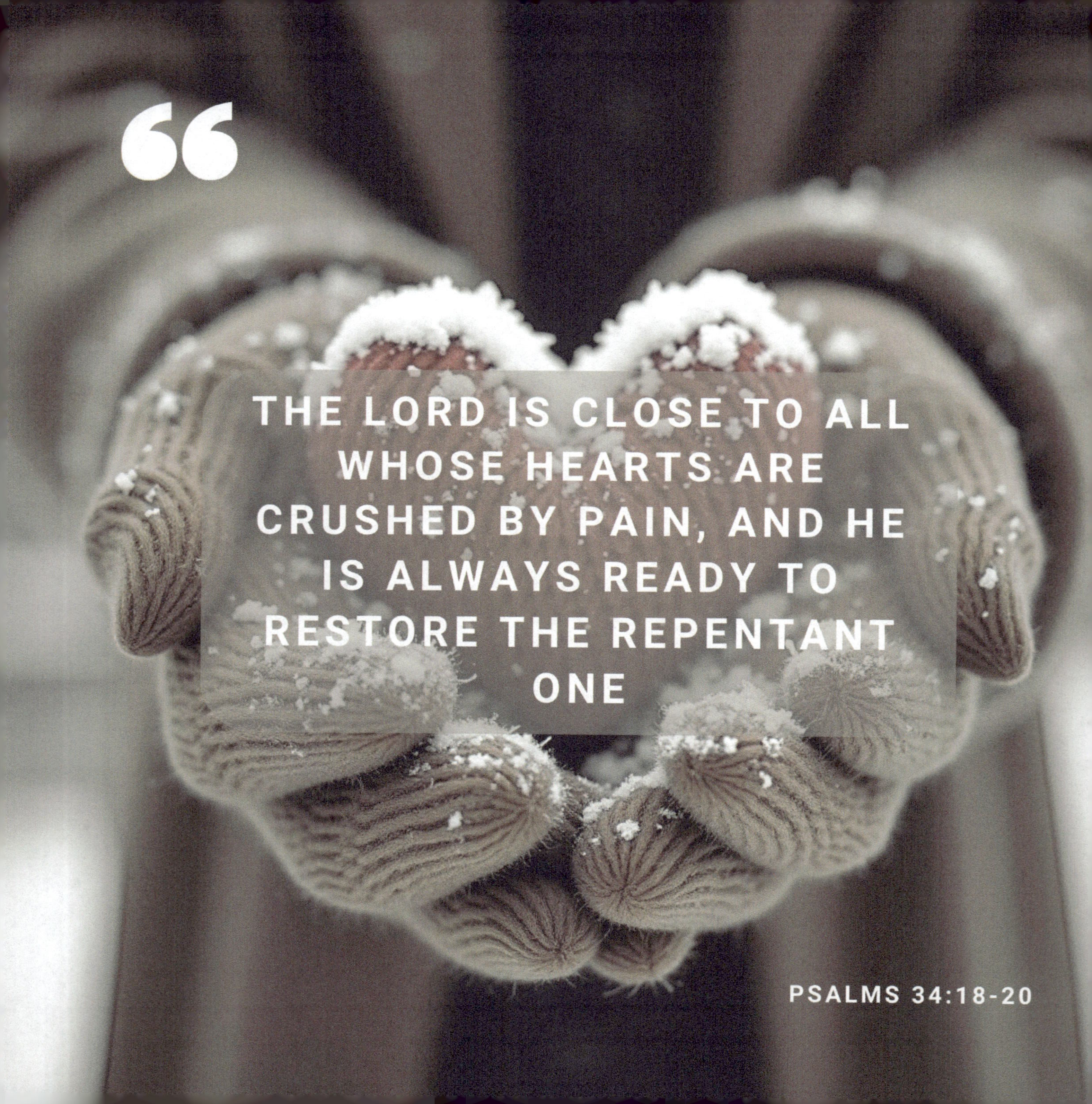
“
THE LORD IS CLOSE TO ALL WHOSE HEARTS ARE CRUSHED BY PAIN, AND HE IS ALWAYS READY TO RESTORE THE REPENTANT ONE
PSALMS 34:18-20

“The Lord is close to all whose hearts are crushed by pain, and He is always ready to restore the repentant one.” Psalm 34:18

Have you ever felt the kind of pain that takes your breath away—the kind of pain that feels as though your heart is being crushed under the weight of sorrow? Crushing pain often sneaks into our lives uninvited through circumstances we never anticipated. It comes in many forms: loss, betrayal, disappointment, or heartbreak. None of us are immune to it, and most of us will experience it at some point in our lives.

In those moments, it can feel as though our hearts are cracked wide open, with raw emotions spilling out—grief, confusion, and despair. But here’s the hope we hold onto: this is His promise—He will be close to us in those moments. He will not leave us to face our pain alone. His nearness is a steadying presence, a reminder that even in our darkest hour, we are held in His love.

The latest heartbreaking moment in my life came when we lost our precious little grandchild. The pain was like nothing I had ever known. When I heard the news, it felt as though the air had been stolen from my lungs. My mind raced with questions I couldn’t answer, and my heart refused to accept the reality. The sorrow was overwhelming, and the helplessness was crushing. I could only imagine the anguish the parents were experiencing, and it broke me even more. I had no words to comfort them with, and we only cried together.

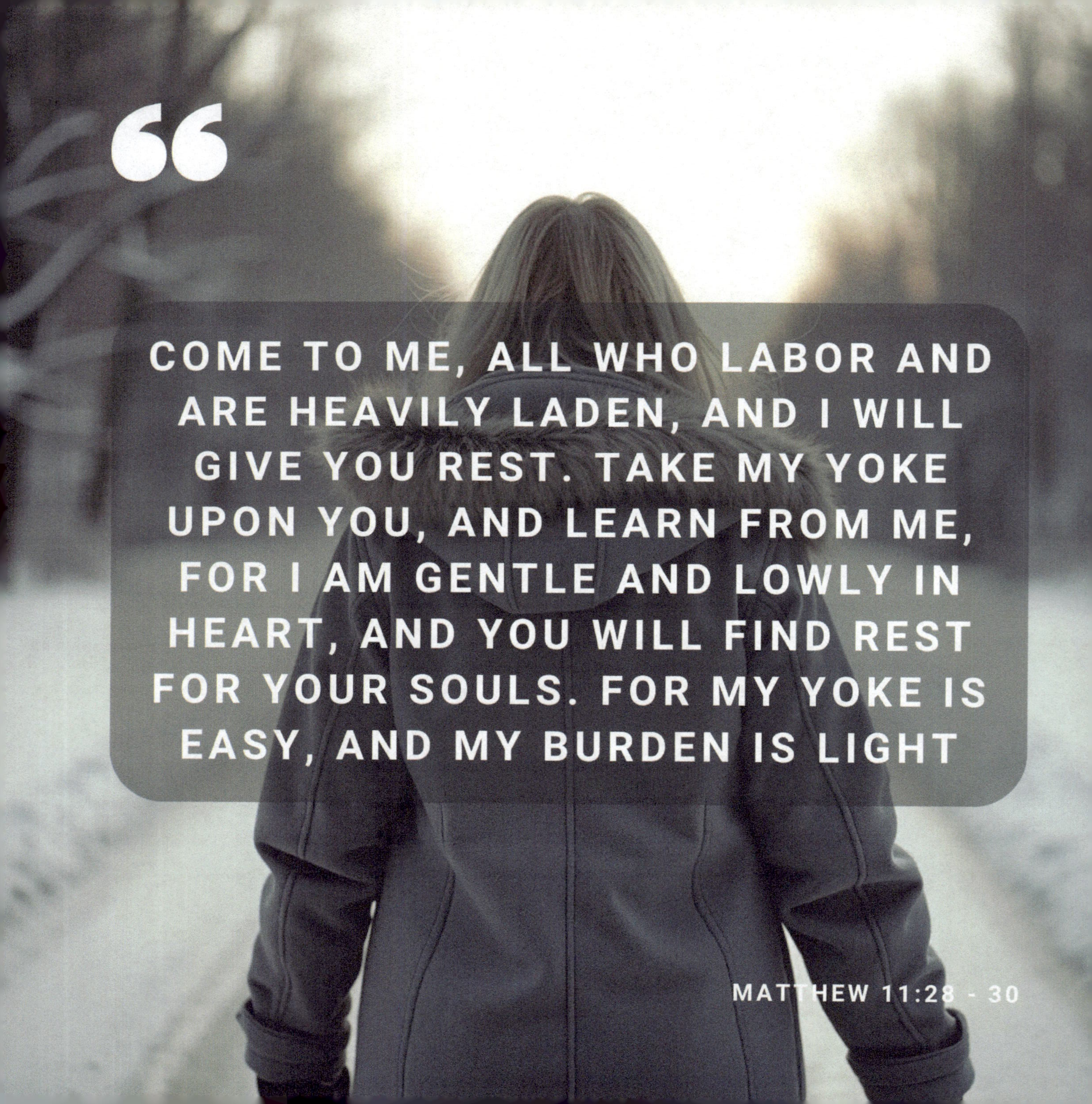
“
COME TO ME, ALL WHO LABOR AND ARE HEAVILY LADEN, AND I WILL GIVE YOU REST. TAKE MY YOKE UPON YOU, AND LEARN FROM ME, FOR I AM GENTLE AND LOWLY IN HEART, AND YOU WILL FIND REST FOR YOUR SOULS. FOR MY YOKE IS EASY, AND MY BURDEN IS LIGHT
MATTHEW 11:28 - 30

In that crushing moment, I had a profound change of heart. Instead of demanding to understand all the "whys" and "hows" of what had happened, I chose to surrender. I placed my trust in the truth that God knows what He is doing, even when I don't, and I accepted that some questions will always remain unanswered. It was a pivotal moment of choice—either I could grow bitter toward God, allowing my pain to create distance, or I could run to Him, seeking His comfort and restoration. I chose to run to Him.

His nearness became my only anchor. He met me in the depths of my sorrow, bringing comfort that defied understanding. Even when words failed, His presence always spoke peace to my heart. This is the God we serve - a God who draws close to the brokenhearted and stays with us in our pain. He doesn't rush us to "move on" or diminish our suffering. Instead, He walks with us right through it, offering restoration in His perfect timing. When the pain feels unbearable, just lean into Him. He is near, He is faithful, and He will not let you walk through it alone. He is all for you. You are loved!

Prayer: Lord, in moments when my heart feels crushed under the weight of sorrow, remind me of Your promise to stay near. Help me to surrender the questions I cannot answer and trust that You are in control, even when life feels chaotic. Draw me closer to You, and let Your presence be my comfort and peace. Restore what is broken in me, and turn my pain into a testimony of your Love and faithfulness. I choose to run to You, Lord, knowing You are always ready to heal and restore. In Jesus' name, Amen.

Sofia

FRENCH DATE CAKE

I DON'T REMEMBER WHY THIS CAKE IS CALLED FRENCH, BUT MY LATE GRANDMOTHER USED TO MAKE IT AND SERVE IT WITH HER BEST CHINA. AS THE SWEET AROMA FILLED HER HOUSE, WE ALL KNEW THAT THE BEST AND MOST ENJOYABLE SEASON WAS FINALLY AT HAND. I MAKE THIS CAKE WHENEVER I MISS MY GRANDMOTHER.

YOU WILL NEED:

1 CUP CHOPPED AND PITTED DATES
1 CUP WATER
2 STICKS OF BUTTER
2 LARGE EGGS
1/2 CUP SUGAR
1TBS VANILLA
1/3 CUP HEAVY CREAM
11/3 CUPS FLOUR
2 TSP BAKING SODA
STAR ANISE (OPTIONAL)
BUTTER AND BREADCRUMBS TO COAT THE CAKE PAN.

TAKE ALL OF THE INGREDIENTS TO ROOM TEMPERATURE A COUPLE OF HOURS BEFORE YOU START BAKING.

START WITH THE CAKE PAN. USE A GENEROUS AMOUNT OF BUTTER AND CREATE A THIN LAYER AROUND THE CAKE PAN. ADD BREAD CRUMBS AND SWIRL THE CAKE PAN AROUND UNTIL IT IS EVENLY COATED.

TAKE THE PITTED AND CHOPPED DATES AND LET SIMMER IN WATER UNTIL SOFT. REMOVE THE PAN FROM THE HEAT AND ADD BUTTER. WHISK UNTIL THE BUTTER HAS MELTED AND THE MIXTURE LOOKS EVEN.

WHIP THE EGGS AND SUGAR UNTIL A FLUFFY WHITE CONSISTENCY IS REACHED. ADD VANILLA AND THE HEAVY CREAM. MIX THE BAKING SODA WITH THE FLOUR AND SIFT IT GENTLY INTO THE EGG MIXTURE. ADD HALF OF THE DATE-BUTTER AND FOLD GENTLY. ADD THE REST OF THE DATE-BUTTER AND SOME GROUND STAR ANISE AND MIX GENTLY UNTIL EVEN.

POUR THE MIXTURE INTO THE EARLIER PREPARED CAKE PAN AND BAKE AT 347F APPROXIMATELY AN HOUR. YOU CAN CHECK IF THE CAKE IS READY IN AN OLD-FASHIONED WAY BY GENTLY INSERTING A TOOTHPICK INTO IT - IF THERE ARE NO CRUMBS ON THE TOOTHPICK WHEN YOU TAKE IT OUT OF THE CAKE, THE CAKE IS READY. TURN THE CAKE AND LET IT COOL COMPLETELY ON A RACK BEFORE CUTTING IT.

SERVE WITH HAPPY MEMORIES!

IN WHAT WAYS DO YOU
FEEL "RICHER" THAN
OTHER PEOPLE?

Money makes people poor; God says it so well. I personally know some of those "rich" who ARE never satisfied, act, or look happy. I was one of them!

In a world filled with shiny objects and extravagant displays of wealth, it can be easy to get caught up in the allure of material possessions. The promising sense of fulfillment and happiness that seems just within reach. I've personally discovered later in my life that true wealth lies not in mansions, cars, or designer clothes but in the richness that comes from within.

As I moved through my life adorned with luxury items, I began to see through the facade of material wealth. The possessions that once seemed so desirable now left me feeling empty, as if they were a poor substitute for the true riches that could be found in the depths of my heart and soul.

Instead of finding happiness in the latest gadgets or fashionable accessories, I found joy in the simple moments of life – a warm smile, a kind gesture, a shared laugh with a friend, or a simple red heart emoji. I realized that true wealth could not be bought or acquired but had to be nurtured and cultivated from within.

“
THE BLESSING OF THE LORD MAKES
A PERSON RICH,
AND HE ADDS NO SORROW WITH IT
PROVERBS 10:22

Slowly, I let go of the need for external validation and embraced the contentment that comes with a grateful heart. I found that in counting my blessings and cherishing real relationships, I discovered a wealth that no amount of money could buy.

When you shift your focus from the outward to the inward, you will find a sense of peace and satisfaction that you never experienced before. You will learn that true happiness lies not in what you have but in who you are with and how you choose to live your life.

And so, embrace a new way of being, one that prioritizes love, peace, compassion, and gratitude above all else. While money can bring temporary comfort, true wealth is found in the depths of your soul.

In the end, I realized that money may make some people extremely poor in spirit, but true richness was always within reach for those who chose to seek it. Strive to live your life by honoring the truest form of wealth – the wealth that could never be taken away, the wealth that resides deep within your heart.

Julia

BITTERSWEET CHOCOLATE POUND CAKE

2 CUPS ALL-PURPOSE FLOUR
1 TEASPOON BAKING SODA
1 TEASPOON BAKING POWDER
1½ CUPS WATER
2 TABLESPOONS INSTANT COFFEE GRANULES
4 BARS (2 OUNCES EACH) NESTLÉ®
UNSWEETENED BAKING
CHOCOLATE, BROKEN UP, DIVIDED
2 CUPS GRANULATED SUGAR
1 CUP (2 STICKS) BUTTER, SOFTENED
1 TEASPOON VANILLA EXTRACT
3 EGGS

CHOCOLATE GLAZE

3 TABLESPOONS BUTTER
1½ CUPS SIFTED POWDERED SUGAR
2 TO 3 TABLESPOONS WATER
1 TEASPOON VANILLA EXTRACT
POWDERED SUGAR (OPTIONAL)

DIRECTIONS

MAKES 12 SERVINGS

FOR CAKE:
COMBINE FLOUR, BAKING SODA, AND BAKING POWDER IN A SMALL BOWL. BRING WATER AND COFFEE TO A BOIL IN A SMALL SAUCEPAN; REMOVE FROM HEAT. ADD 3 BARS (6 OUNCES) OF BAKING CHOCOLATE; STIR UNTIL SMOOTH.

BEAT SUGAR, BUTTER, AND VANILLA IN A LARGE MIXING BOWL UNTIL CREAMY. ADD EGGS; BEAT ON HIGH SPEED FOR 5 MINUTES. BEAT IN THE FLOUR MIXTURE ALTERNATELY WITH THE CHOCOLATE MIXTURE. POUR INTO A WELL-GREASED 10-INCH BUNDT PAN.

BAKE IN A PREHEATED 325°F OVEN FOR 50 TO 60 MINUTES UNTIL A LONG WOODEN PICK INSERTED INTO THE CENTER OF THE CAKE COMES OUT CLEAN. COOL IN THE PAN ON A WIRE RACK FOR 30 MINUTES. REMOVE FROM PAN; COOL COMPLETELY. DRIZZLE WITH CHOCOLATE GLAZE; SPRINKLE WITH POWDERED SUGAR.

FOR CHOCOLATE GLAZE:
MELT THE REMAINING BAKING BAR (2 OUNCES) AND BUTTER IN A SMALL, HEAVY SAUCEPAN OVER LOW HEAT, STIRRING UNTIL SMOOTH.

REMOVE FROM HEAT. STIR IN POWDERED SUGAR ALTERNATELY WITH WATER UNTIL DESIRED CONSISTENCY. STIR IN VANILLA.

CHOOSE PEACE. NOT THE
KIND THE WORLD GIVES
BUT THE ONE THAT
COMES FROM OUR
HEAVENLY FATHER

"I leave the gift of peace with you - my peace. Not the kind of fragile peace given by the world, but my perfect peace. Don´t yield to fear or be troubled in your hearts - instead, be courageous!"

What a timely and special word that is! I am reminded of this every single time I see the news or scroll through social media. It is as if we are surrounded with only troubles, and not a day goes by without some kind of new bad news emerging. Wars, rumors of wars, earthquakes, and collapses of economies. What is important to remember is that WE don´t need to fear anything - we are always safe and secure in Christ Jesus, our Saviour. In the midst of all the trouble, we can choose the Prince of Peace.

I have experienced that with the Word of God; it is not enough to just hear it. We have to hear it, apply it, and then continuously practice it until we become masters in using it. We can also always ask for wisdom when going through challenging times. We have to let the Word of God renew our minds. Sometimes, our thoughts are simply restless. We let our thoughts run all over the place until we start feeling anxious about the future. It is easy to see why Jesus told His disciples and us so many times: "Fear not!"

What stands out to me in this passage is that Jesus knew very well that the peace of this world would be only temporary and very fragile. What does it mean? Simply, we can not place our trust in it because it will not last.

CIRCUMSTANCES WILL CHANGE

The peace of this world is placed more often than not on all kinds of possessions and on people of power. Possessions rust, decay, and disappear, and even the most loyal friends may leave and betray you. The peace Jesus gives to us, however, is steadfast and strong. It is like a rock. It does not change. It does not move. We can place our trust in it. If God said it, that is what will happen. "I give you peace!"

I remember when I first read this Bible passage so vividly. For a moment there, I thought to myself that the peace would come because the circumstances would immediately, miraculously change. If the troubles and challenges would stop in a mysterious way, I could find peace. I was striving to get rid of the problems as soon as possible. I was desperately trying to change my circumstances so that I could finally experience peace.

The beauty of it all is, though, that He gives us peace in the middle of all the chaos. He gives us peace, although everything looks hopeless and messy. It is a bit like it is said that in the middle of hurricane winds, there remains a calm spot in the center. The world may rage, but we can remain calm and experience perfect peace in Him. There is also something miraculous in the way He gives us peace, and we can choose to be courageous and fearless, regardless of our current circumstances. What ever it looks like now, God will see you through!

Sofia

PS. Jesus slept in a storm!

GIVE YOURSELF PERMISSION
TO ENJOY A MOMENT OF BLISS

COFFEE WITH BANANA CREAM

WHEN IT IS COLD AND DARK OUTSIDE, IT IS WONDERFUL TO HAVE SOMETHING HOT AND TASTY TO ENJOY. THIS DRINK IS A BIT CRAZY SUBSTITUTE TO THE DRINKS WITH ALCOHOL, BUT IT IS FUN TO MAKE AND LOOKS FANCY. IT TASTES GOOD, TOO, ESPECIALLY AFTER A LONG WALK IN THE WOODS.

YOU WILL NEED:

- 2 SHOTS ESPRESSO
- 1 CUP HOT FROTHED MILK
- 1/2 BANANA
- CHOCOLATE SAUCE OR HONEY, PECAN NUTS
- WHIPPED CREAM (OPTIONAL, BUT GREAT FUN)

TAKE THE FANCIEST MUGS OR GLASSES THAT YOU HAPPEN TO HAVE (THEY HAVE TO TOLERATE HOT LIQUID). SWIRL SOME CHOCOLATE SAUCE OR HONEY ON THE SIDES OF THE GLASS FOR ADDED FLAVOR.

MAKE DOUBLE ESPRESSO AND FROTH THE MILK. POUR HALF OF THE MILK OVER THE ESPRESSO SHOTS AND BLITZ THE OTHER HALF WITH BANANA IN A BLENDER. POUR GENTLY OVER COFFEE. GARNISH WITH WHIPPED CREAM, THIN BANANA SLICES, A FEW PECAN NUT PIECES, AND SOME CHOCOLATE SAUCE.

PRO TIP: ENJOY SLOWLY, SAVORING EACH SIP WATCHING THE SNOW FALL.

ENJOY THE GIFT
peace

Peace is a word that holds significant importance in the Christian faith. It goes beyond the absence of conflict or turmoil, reflecting a state of wholeness, harmony, and tranquility.

It is a deep and abiding sense of wholeness, harmony, and well-being that is rooted in God's love and grace. Through a personal relationship with God, believers can experience His peace in all circumstances, knowing that it surpasses all understanding and guards their hearts and minds. As we meditate on the verses that speak of God's peace, may we be encouraged to embrace this gift and allow it to reign in our lives, bringing glory to God and blessing to others.

The Bible also teaches that God's peace is available to believers even in the midst of trials and tribulations. Philippians 4:6-7 encourages believers, "Do not be anxious about anything, but in every situation, by prayer and petition, with thanksgiving, present your requests to God. And the peace of God, which transcends all understanding, will guard your hearts and your minds in Christ Jesus." This Bible verse reminds us that when we bring our worries and concerns to God in prayer, His peace will guard our hearts and minds, providing comfort and strength even in difficult times.

Peace.

“
FOR THE WAGES OF SIN IS DEATH, BUT THE GIFT OF GOD IS ETERNAL LIFE IN CHRIST JESUS OUR LORD.
ROMANS 6:23

As we prepare to celebrate the upcoming holiday season amidst the swirling rush of decorating trees, baking cookies, and shopping for gifts, take time to pause and reflect on the true reason behind this festive time of year. At the center of all the festivities, Jesus Christ stands as the most precious gift we could ever receive.

The birth of Jesus Christ marks the beginning of a new era, a promise of hope, love, and salvation for all who believe. In a world full of turmoil and sin, Jesus came to show us a better way. In the Old Testament, people were required to make sacrifices to atone for their sins, but God, in His infinite mercy and grace, sent His only Son to be the ultimate sacrifice for us all.

Jesus walked among us, experiencing the same trials and tribulations that we face in our daily lives. He showed us the path to overcoming worldly temptations, the importance of self-control, the power of forgiveness, and the depth of true love. His teachings and example have served as a guiding light for countless generations, inspiring us to live with compassion, humility, and grace.

As we gather with loved ones and exchange gifts this holiday season, let us rejoice in the birth of our Savior - JESUS CHRIST!

Julia

A LITTLE
CHRISTMAS
MIRACLE

One year, the days leading up to Christmas seemed to blur into a whirlwind of activity, and before we knew it, Christmas Eve had arrived—and we had no tree. It wasn't intentional; life had simply gotten ahead of us. Determined not to let Christmas pass without the warm glow of a beautifully adorned tree, my daughter and I decided to fix the situation.

We set out together, confident we could find a tree on our way home. Surely, even on Christmas Eve, there would still be trees available. But shop after shop dashed our hopes—each one had already sold out. By the time we reached the third store with nothing to show for our efforts, desperation started to creep in. The hours of Christmas Eve were quickly ticking away, and It seemed as though our chances of finding a tree were as dim as the winter sky.

Feeling the weight of disappointment, we paused in the car, and my daughter and I did something simple but profound—we prayed. "Papa, help!" We whispered a heartfelt plea to our heavenly father. It wasn't eloquent or long-winded, just a childlike call for help.

As we turned the next corner, something caught our eye: a small Christmas tree lot, its lights still glowing. We couldn't believe it! The lot had escaped our notice all evening, and yet here it was, tucked away as if waiting just for us.

ONLY ONE PERFECT TREE LEFT

We hurried over, our hearts pounding with cautious hope. A man was packing up his gear, clearly ready to close for the night. Only a couple of trees remained, and as we examined them, our eyes fell on one that was perfect—exactly what we'd been hoping for.

The man, kind and cheerful despite the late hour, helped us load the tree onto our car. As we drove away, the feeling of relief and gratitude washed over us. But there was something more. My daughter and I looked at each other, sharing the same thought without saying it aloud: it felt as though this tree lot had been there just for us.

As the car carried us home, the wonder of the moment settled into our hearts. Could it be that we'd just experienced a little Christmas miracle? It certainly felt that way. We half-joked that if we turned the car around and tried to find that lot again, it might not even be there.

That tree became more than just part of our Christmas decorations—it was a constant reminder of God's love and attentiveness. Every time we looked at it, we found ourselves smiling. It wasn't just a tree; it was a symbol of hope, provision, and the joy of a Father who cares about even the smallest details of our lives.

NO PRAYER IS TOO SMALL, AND NO MOMENT IS TOO ORDINARY FOR GOD TO WORK A LITTLE MIRACLE.

To this day, it remains the most beautiful Christmas tree we've ever had, not because of its size or shape but because it came wrapped in the unmistakable gift of God's grace. It was a moment of divine kindness that turned an ordinary Christmas Eve into an unforgettable memory.

Sometimes, we forget that God delights in surprising us. He meets us not just in our grandest needs but in our simplest ones, reminding us that He sees, hears, and loves us. That year, a humble Christmas tree reminded us of a profound truth: no prayer is too small, and no moment too ordinary for God to work a little miracle.

Sofia

NEW YEAR ROAST BEEF

INGREDIENTS

- 1(3 POUND) ROUND ROAST
- 1/4 CUP EXTRA-VIRGIN OLIVE OIL
- 4 CLOVES GARLIC, MINCED
- 2 TABLESPOONS FRESH ROSEMARY, CHOPPED
- 2 TABLESPOONS FRESH THYME LEAVES, CHOPPED
- 1-2 TEASPOONS KOSHER SALT
- 1 TEASPOON GROUND BLACK PEPPER

DIRECTIONS

PREHEAT THE OVEN TO 450 DEGREES F.

IN A BOWL, COMBINE THE OLIVE OIL, THE GARLIC, THE ROSEMARY, THE THYME, THE SALT, AND THE PEPPER.

RUB THE SEASONING MIXTURE OVER ALL THE SIDES OF THE ROOM-TEMPERATURE ROAST.

PLACE THE ROAST IN A ROASTING PAN AND ROAST IT FOR 15 MINUTES.

REDUCE THE HEAT TO 325 DEGREES F.

ROAST UNTIL MEDIUM, READING 140 DEGREES F ON A THERMOMETER, ABOUT 1 HOUR 45 MINUTES.

REMOVE THE ROAST FROM THE OVEN AND LET IT SLIGHTLY COOL FOR ABOUT 15-30 MINUTES.

SERVE WARM, AND ENJOY!

“
FOR GOD SEES EVERYTHING YOU DO, AND HIS EYES ARE WIDE OPEN AS HE OBSERVES EVERY SINGLE HABIT YOU HAVE
PROVERBS 5:21-23

Imagine if we lived in transparent homes, where honesty prevailed as actions were laid bare for all to see. Maybe kindness and faith would be the only shining light in those houses filled with the power of love and integrity. If people knew that behind closed doors, they are being watched 24/7. Perhaps the transparency would inspire them to behave better and make a positive change. The cities and villages would be transformed into a community of love and acceptance, showcasing the importance of being true to ourselves, as nothing is hidden from God's watchful eyes. As a true believer, you already know that we don't need to live in aquariums to make those changes because nothing is hidden from God, and He can see us no matter how thick or thin our walls are, no matter how many locks on the door or lightproof curtains we have. He sees through us, staring at our hearts' motives.

Start now; it's never too late. Treat others with respect and compassion. Live your life in a way that reflects your deep faith in God and His belief in the power of love. Constantly remind yourself that nothing is hidden, not even your thoughts. Everything is laid bare for God to witness.

God's eyes are always watching, whether behind walls or in full view. The words of Proverbs 15:3,

"The eyes of the Lord are in every place, keeping watch on the evil and the good."

YOU WILL SHOW ME THE WAY OF LIFE, GRANTING ME THE JOY OF YOUR PRESENCE AND THE PLEASURES OF LIVING WITH YOU FOREVER
PSALM 16:11

PARTY PLATTER

SNACK LAVISHLY WITH A DECADENT GRAZING BOARD.

FROM THE CRUNCHY STAR-SHAPED SNACKS TO THE SAVORY OLIVES AND CHARCUTERIE ROSES. THIS GRAZING BOARD WILL BE THE MOST POPULAR THING ON YOUR HOLIDAY TABLE. THOUGH IT LOOKS IMPRESSIVE, IT'S A CINCH TO MAKE!

TO DO: START WITH YOUR BOARD'S ANCHORS:

PLACE BLOCKS OF CHEESE ON A LARGE ROUND TRAY ALONG WITH CRACKERS AND OLIVES. CREATE ONE OR TWO "RIVERS" BY LINING UP CUT CHEESE SLICES, ROLLED MEATS, AND GRAPES ON THE BOARD. FILL GAPS WITH OTHER FRUITS, VEGGIES, SALAMI.

"ROSES" AND NUTS (OPTIONAL). TUCK IN HERBS.

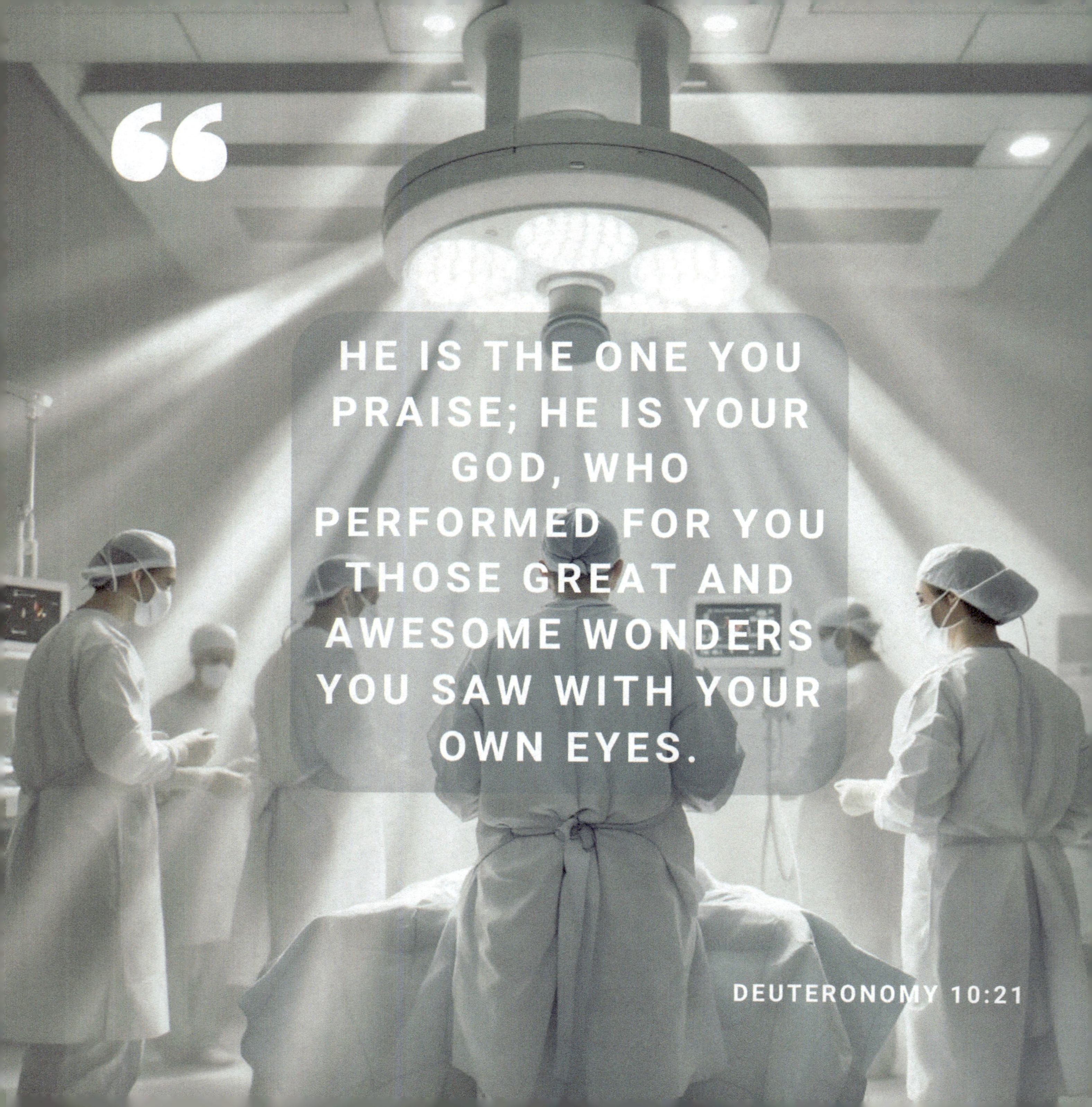
“
HE IS THE ONE YOU PRAISE; HE IS YOUR GOD, WHO PERFORMED FOR YOU THOSE GREAT AND AWESOME WONDERS YOU SAW WITH YOUR OWN EYES.
DEUTERONOMY 10:21

Do you believe in miracles? I do. Sometimes, they happen quickly and unexpectedly, and sometimes, it takes time to recognize God is doing His thing. I've seen and heard so many times about couples who couldn't have children, but after praying for a miracle, they have been blessed to make it happen.

A year ago, as my family and I were celebrating my mother's birthday, my father had a heart attack. I still remember that feeling sitting next to him in the ambulance and hearing the nurse tell me that he was in the middle of a heart attack and might not make it to the hospital. That devastated and helpless feeling was so intense and painful that I will never forget it.

There was nobody to comfort me but God. I was praying as never before. I knew God was there, and He was the only one who could turn things around and perform a miracle. I ended up next to my father in the surgery room and personally saw the entire process of an amazing medical staff. They worried about making everything right and worked hard trying to save my father. I stood speechless, watching my beloved daddy fighting for his life. Time stood still; I wanted to be there instead of him. As I'm writing this and re-living those moments in my mind, those worries I went through, I can't hold back my tears.

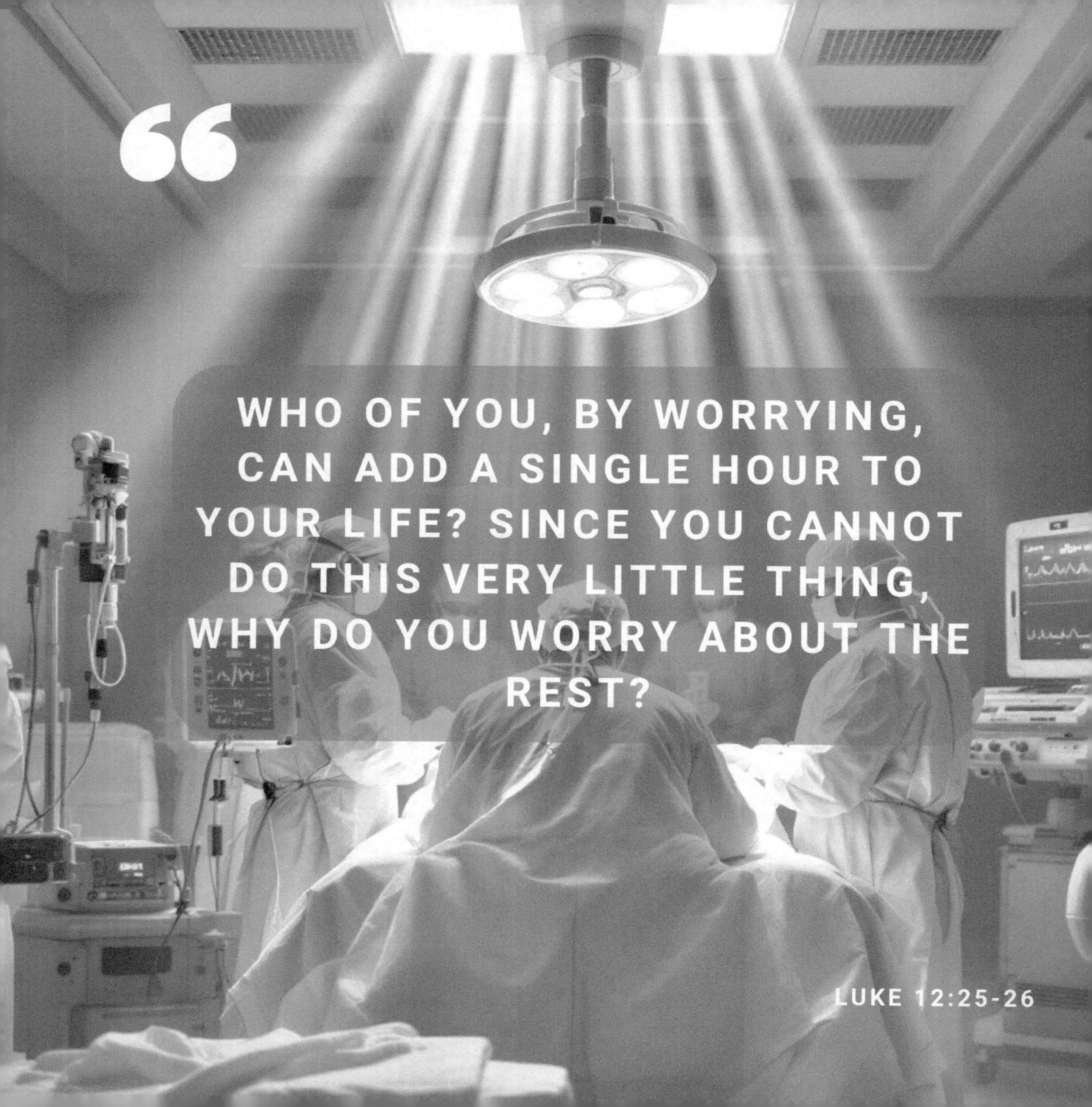
“
WHO OF YOU, BY WORRYING, CAN ADD A SINGLE HOUR TO YOUR LIFE? SINCE YOU CANNOT DO THIS VERY LITTLE THING, WHY DO YOU WORRY ABOUT THE REST?
LUKE 12:25-26

God gave mercy to the entire family, restored his heart, and brought my father back home to us and his beloved wife of 55 years. I'm endlessly grateful for the main Doctor who is in control of my father's life. He asked us in Luke 12:25-26:

"Who of you, by worrying, can add a single hour to your life? Since you cannot do this very little thing, why do you worry about the rest?"

There's another reminder to all of us in Deuteronomy 31:6:

"Be strong and courageous. Do not be afraid or terrified because of them, for the LORD your God goes with you; he will never leave you nor forsake you."

Thank you, Lord!

Julia

NEW YEAR BERRY BAKE

INGREDIENTS

- 21/2 CUPS PLUS 1/3 CUP ALL-PURPOSE FLOUR, DIVIDED, PLUS MORE, TO TASTE, FOR DUSTING A WORK SURFACE
- 13/4 TEASPOONS BAKING POWDER
- 3/4 TEASPOON SALT
- 1/2 CUP SHORTENING
- 2/3 CUP MILK
- 2 CUPS PLUS 1 TABLESPOON SUGAR, DIVIDED
- 1 TEASPOON FRESH LEMON JUICE
- 2(16-OUNCE) PACKAGES FROZEN BLACKBERRIES
- 1/4 CUP BUTTER, CUT INTO 1/4-INCH PIECES, DIVIDED
- VANILLA ICE CREAM, OPTIONAL, TO TASTE, FOR SERVING
- OPTIONAL: USE COOKIE CUTTERS FOR STARS OR ANY OTHER SHAPES

DIRECTIONS

PREHEAT THE OVEN TO 425 DEGREES F.

LIGHTLY GREASE A BAKING SHEET AND A 9X13-INCH BAKING DISH.

IN A BOWL, ADD 2 1/2 CUPS OF FLOUR, BAKING POWDER, AND THE SALT. MIX ALL THE INGREDIENTS TOGETHER.

ADD PRE-CUT SHORTENING AND THE FLOUR MIXTURE INTO THE BLENDER AND MIX IT UNTIL ALL OF THE INGREDIENTS ARE SLIGHTLY CRUMBLED.

ADD THE MILK TO THE FLOUR MIXTURE AND STIR UNTIL ALL OF THE DRY INGREDIENTS ARE MOISTENED AND THE MIXTURE IS SOFT ENOUGH TO FORM INTO A SOFT BALL.

LIGHTLY DUST A WORK SURFACE WITH THE EXTRA FLOUR, KNEAD THE DOUGH ABOUT EIGHT TIMES ON THE PREPARED SURFACE, AND DIVIDE IT IN HALF.

ROLL 1 DOUGH HALF TO 1/4-INCH THICKNESS AND CUT IT INTO 1-INCH-WIDE STRIPS.

PLACE THE DOUGH STRIPS ONTO THE PREPARED BAKING SHEET.

BAKE IT UNTIL LIGHTLY BROWNED, ABOUT 10-15 MINUTES.

NOBODY'S GOIN TO DO
YOUR LIFE FOR YOU,
YOU HAVE TO DO IT YOURSELF

TRANSFER THE STRIPS TO A WIRE RACK TO COOL COMPLETELY FOR ABOUT 30 MINUTES.

REDUCE THE OVEN TEMPERATURE TO 350 DEGREES.

ROLL THE REMAINING DOUGH HALF TO 1/4-INCH THICKNESS.

CUT THE DOUGH INTO 1-INCH-WIDE STRIPS.

IN A LARGE BOWL, ADD 2 CUPS OF SUGAR, THE REMAINING 1/3 CUP OF FLOUR, THE LEMON JUICE, AND THE FROZEN BLACKBERRIES, AND GENTLY MIX TO COMBINE.

SPOON 1/2 OF THE BLACKBERRY MIXTURE INTO THE PREPARED BAKING DISH.

BREAK EACH OF THE BAKED DOUGH STRIPS INTO 2-3 PIECES.

PLACE THE BAKED DOUGH PIECES ON TOP OF THE BLACKBERRY MIXTURE LAYER.

DOT THE BLACKBERRY MIXTURE LAYER WITH 1/2 OF THE BUTTER PIECES.

SPOON THE REMAINING BLACKBERRY MIXTURE OVER THE BAKED DOUGH AND THE BUTTER LAYER.

ARRANGE THE UNBAKED DOUGH STRIPS (OPTIONAL: IN A LATTICE DESIGN) OVER THE FILLING.

THE BEAUTY OF ENDINGS
IS THAT THEY LEAD TO
NEW BEGINNINGS
New Year

SPRINKLE THE DOUGH STRIPS WITH THE REMAINING 1 TABLESPOON OF SUGAR.

DOT THE BLACKBERRY MIXTURE WITH THE REMAINING BUTTER PIECES.

BAKE UNTIL THE PASTRY ON TOP IS GOLDEN AND THE MIXTURE IS BUBBLY, ABOUT 50 MINUTES AND 1 HOUR.

SERVE WITH THE VANILLA ICE CREAM.

ENJOY!

JANUARY

CHAPTER 2

GOD'S VOICE IS GLORIOUS IN THE THUNDER. WE CAN'T EVEN IMAGINE THE GREATNESS OF HIS POWER. HE DIRECTS THE SNOW TO FALL ON THE EARTH AND TELLS THE RAIN TO POUR DOWN

JOB 37:5-6

EVERY DAY IS A
NEW BEGINNING

12:00 January 1st in most countries it's a new beginning. New year. New opportunities. New goals. New dreams. New ideas. New times!

Time is the most powerful force in the Universe.

Every passing second there are twenty-four thousand tons of ice melted, 4 babies are born, 2 people die, and earth moves 18 1/2 miles through space. 60 seconds in every minute, 60 minutes in every hour, and then 24 hours per day gives us more than 31 million seconds in a year.

Let's observe how much unfolds for us this year!

Nobody can control time. Nobody can stop it, but we all worry about it, while Luke 12:25-26 reminds us "You cannot add any time to your life by worrying about it. If you cannot do even the little things, then why worry about the big things?"

The Lord's perspective on time is different from that of humans. He doesn't need time. Indeed, He doesn't have it. He's eternal. He has no beginning and no end. Isn't that amazing? You could say He's the original time traveler, always present, past, and future simultaneously.

REMEMBER:
YOUR CAPACITY FOR LOVE AND COMPASSION MAKE THE WORLD A BETTER PLACE

As we step into the new year, let's embrace the Christian life with faith and hope. Let's allow God's timeless wisdom to guide us through the days ahead. Our journey with God is not bound by the constraints of time, for His love and grace are eternal.

Let's remember that God walks alongside us every step of the way, and He has a plan for us. Jeremiah 29:11, "For I know the plans I have for you," declares the Lord, "plans to prosper you and not to harm you, plans to give you hope and a future."

Julia

WHERE TO START?
NEW
GOALS

So, where do we begin in our new year's journey? What is the first and perhaps the most crucial step to our success? There have been so many stories of people who relied on their own understanding and believed they had it all until they failed. We all have experienced it in one way or another.

One man was rushing out the door to seal the deal of his life, only to discover his car wouldn't start. Consequently, his day was ruined, filled with frustration and anger, as was his important meeting. Little did he know that on a busy intersection where he was supposed to drive, a deadly car crash had occurred, and he could have been one of its victims. Little did he know that the company he was eager to strike a deal with went bankrupt a few months later. All he saw was his broken car and a missed "opportunity," while God saw the bigger picture and provided a better path and a better way to succeed in his future.

Let's seek God's wisdom, not our own, and trust Him in all our endeavors. "But seek first His kingdom and His righteousness, and all these things will be added unto you," Matthew 6:33.

Julia

OUR VERY LIVES ARE
MEANT TO CARRY THE
FRAGRANCE OF HIS LOVE,
GRACE, AND TRUTH

Imagine walking into a room filled with the scent of fresh flowers or warm bread just out of the oven. Instantly, the atmosphere changes. Scents have the power to comfort, refresh, and draw us in. They awaken something deep within us, reminding us of beauty, home, or a cherished moment. The Apostle Paul writes in 2 Corinthians 2:15 that we, as followers of Jesus, are the "aroma of Christ" to God among those being saved. What a profound thought—that our very lives are meant to carry the fragrance of His love, grace, and truth wherever we go.

This heavenly fragrance is an overflow of Jesus living in us. As we spend time with Him—abiding in His love, meditating on His Word, and allowing His Spirit to work in our hearts—we naturally begin to reflect His presence.

The aroma of Christ is not loud or artificial. It doesn't demand attention, yet it's impossible to ignore. It lingers in acts of kindness, words of encouragement, and moments of grace that flow from a heart transformed by God. It's found in the quiet forgiveness we extend when wronged, in the compassion we show to those in need, and in the unwavering joy we carry even in the midst of trials. This fragrance is unique because it points not to us but to Him—it draws others to the beauty of Jesus.

Think about how subtle yet powerful a fragrance can be. It doesn't need to shout or push; it simply exists, and its presence changes the environment. In the same way, our lives, filled with the Spirit of God, can influence others without us even realizing it. May our lives be a reminder of His goodness, a reflection of His love, and a fragrant offering that brings glory to God and draws others closer to Him.

Sofia

LIFE IS LIKE A
CINNAMON BUN,
SWEET AND FULL OF TWISTS

CINNAMON BUNS

I FIRST DISCOVERED THIS VERSION OF CINNAMON BUNS WHILE LIVING IN SWEDEN. THEY'RE A BIT SWEETER THAN THE ONES I USED TO MAKE, AND THEY EMBODY HYGGE IN EVERY BITE—A TRUE COMFORT FOR THE SOUL.

HERE'S A FUN FACT: IN FINLAND, CINNAMON BUNS ARE TYPICALLY SERVED TO CHILDREN WITH COLD MILK, WHILE IN SWEDEN, THEY'RE PAIRED WITH A REFRESHING STRAWBERRY-RASPBERRY JUICE. THE SWEDES EVEN HAVE A CHARMING SAYING ABOUT LIFE: "LIFE IS LIKE CINNAMON BUNS AND JUICE.

YOU WILL NEED:

- 1 AND 1/4 CUP LUKEWARM MILK
- 1 TABLESPOON YEAST
- 1/2 CUP SUGAR
- 1 TEASPOON SALT
- 1 TABLESPOON GROUND CARDAMOM
- 1/4 CUP BUTTER, CUT INTO 4 CHUNKS
- 3 EGGS, 1 EGG RESERVED FOR GLAZE
- 4 1/2 CUPS ALL PURPOSE FLOUR
- CINNAMON & SUGAR & BUTTER

WARM THE MILK AND ADD SUGAR AND 1 TABLESPOON OF YEAST. STIR GENTLY AND LET IT SIT FOR A WHILE. ADD SALT AND EGGS AND MIX UNTIL EVEN. CONTINUE WITH FLOUR AND BUTTER, KNEADING CONTINUOUSLY UNTIL EVEN DOUGH APPEARS. LET REST FOR 30 MINUTES.

HERE IS HOW TO DO IT:

WARM THE MILK GENTLY. ADD SUGAR AND 1 TABLESPOON OF YEAST. STIR UNTIL THE SUGAR HAS MELTED, AND LET THE MIXTURE SIT FOR A WHILE UNTIL YOU SEE BUBBLES ON THE SURFACE (THE YEAST HAS BEEN ACTIVATED). ADD SALT AND EGGS AND MIX UNTIL EVEN. CONTINUE WITH FLOUR AND BUTTER, KNEADING CONTINUOUSLY UNTIL EVEN DOUGH IS FORMED. IT SHOULD NOT STICK TO YOUR FINGERS ANYMORE. LET THE DOUGH REST FOR 30 MINUTES.

PLACE ON LIGHTLY FLOURED SURFACE. ROLL INTO A RECTANGLE OF CHOICE. BUTTER EVENLY AND ADD SUGAR AND CINNAMON TO TASTE. REMEMBER THIS IS ART. ROLL THE DOUGH AND CUT BUNS - TRY TO MAKE THEM EQUAL IN SIZE. PLACE THE CINNAMON BUNS ON A PARCHMENT-COVERED BAKING SHEET. LIGHTLY COVER WITH CLEAN KITCHEN TOWEL AND LET RISE FOR ABOUT 30-45 MINUTES.

PREHEAT OVEN TO 325 DEGREES. BEAT THE REMAINING EGG AND GENTLY BRUSH ON THE TOP AND SIDES OF EACH BUN WITH PASTRY BRUSH. BAKE FOR 10 TO 15 MINUTES UNTIL GOLDEN BROWN. COOL SLIGHTLY ON WIRE RACK AND ENJOY. THESE TASTE BEST HOT RIGHT FROM THE OVEN!

PRO TIP: CINNAMON BUNS FREEZE EXCELLENTLY, AND YOU CAN ENJOY A MOMENT OF HYGGE ANY TIME YOU LIKE.

BUT IF THEY DO NOT WASH THEIR CLOTHES AND BATHE THEMSELVES, THEY WILL BE HELD RESPONSIBLE
LEVITICUS 17:16

THE WINTER SEASON CAN BE A TIME OF HUSTLE AS THE HOLIDAY FESTIVITIES AND COLDER WEATHER CONSUME OUR TIME AND ENERGY.

TAKE YOUR TIME TO RELAX. TAKE A BATH AND USE ESSENTIAL OILS. IS NOT ONLY A DELIGHTFUL WAY TO UNWIND, BUT MANY OF THEM HAVE IMMUNE-BOOSTING, MOOD-ENHANCING, AND STRESS-RELIEVING EFFECTS, MAKING THEM IDEAL COMPANIONS DURING THE WINTER MONTHS.

IN LEVITICUS 17:16, THE EMPHASIS IS ON CLEANLINESS AND PURITY.
OVERALL, THIS VERSE EMPHASIZES THE SIGNIFICANCE OF FOLLOWING RELIGIOUS LAWS AND MAINTAINING CLEANLINESS AS A PART OF ONE'S SPIRITUAL PRACTICE.

INTERESTINGLY, THE IMPORTANCE OF ESSENTIAL OILS IS MENTIONED IN THE BIBLE. IN THE VERSE HEBREWS 1:8–9, GOD SAID TO HAVE ANOINTED JESUS WITH THE "OIL OF GLADNESS."

THEY HAVE BEEN USED FOR THEIR THERAPEUTIC AND AROMATIC PROPERTIES FOR THOUSANDS OF YEARS. SOME ESSENTIAL OILS LIKE MYRRH, HYSSOP, AND FRANKINCENSE WERE USED FOR THEIR HEALING PROPERTIES IN BIBLICAL TIMES (JAMES 5:14).

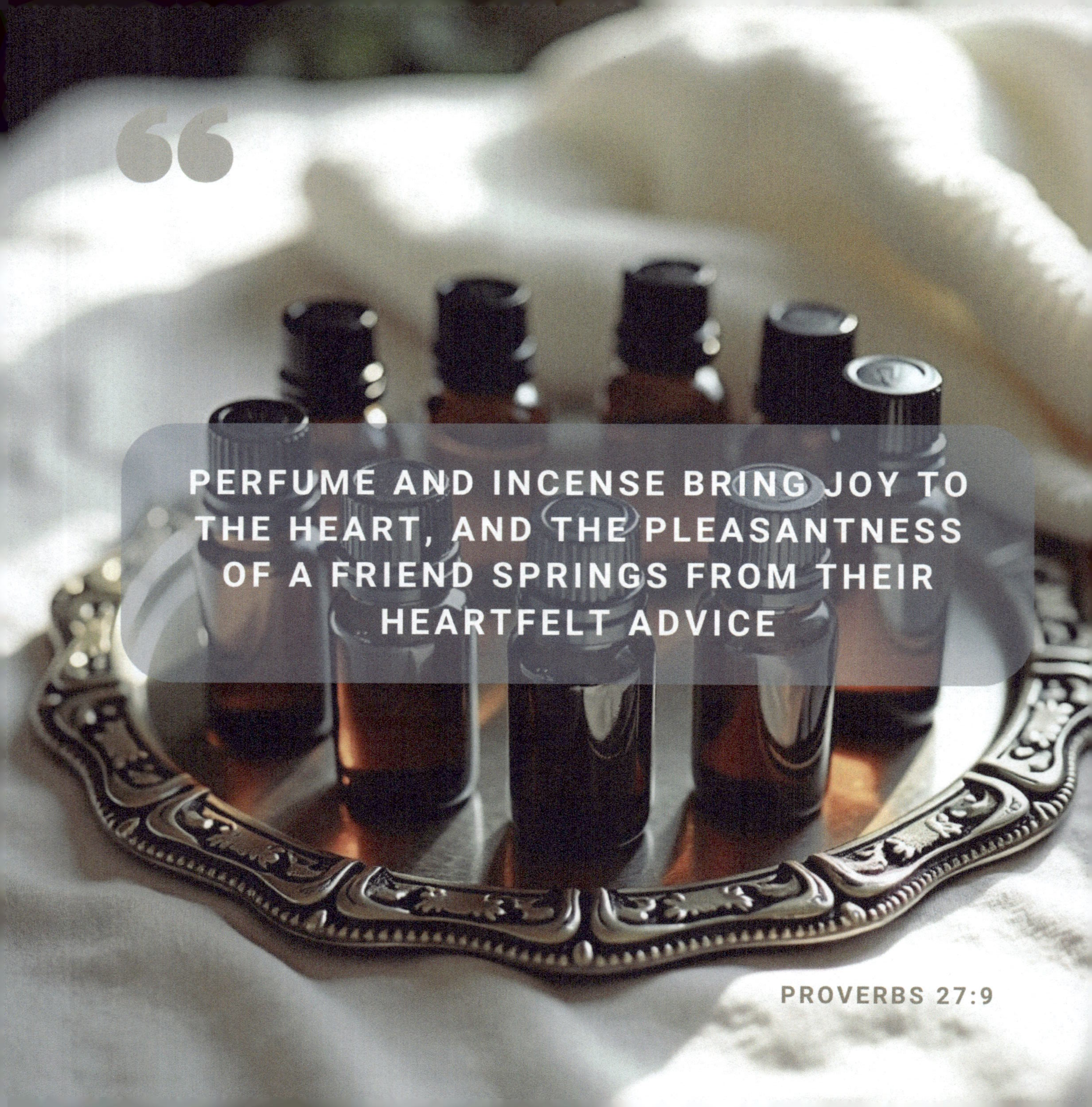
“
PERFUME AND INCENSE BRING JOY TO THE HEART, AND THE PLEASANTNESS OF A FRIEND SPRINGS FROM THEIR HEARTFELT ADVICE
PROVERBS 27:9

Basil: Uplifting, clarifies thought processes

Bergamot: Uplifting, yet calming

Cedarwood: Relaxing, stress-reducing

Chamomile: Soothing and calming

Eucalyptus: Invigorating, cleansing

Fennel: Calming, warming

Fir needle: Refreshing, cleansing

Frankincense: Calming helps release fear

Geranium: Balancing mood swings, harmonizing

Juniper: Purifying, stimulating

Lavender: Calming, soothing, relaxing

Lemon: Uplifting, refreshing

Lemongrass: Stimulating, cleansing, tonifying

Marjoram: Very relaxing, anxiety-reducing

Myrrh: Strengthening, inspiring

Orange: Uplifting, refreshing

Patchouli: Inspiring, sensuous

Peppermint: Stimulating, cleansing, refreshing

Pine: Refreshing, cleansing

Rose: Emotionally soothing, sensuous

Rosemary: Stimulating, invigorating

Sage: Cleansing, purifying

Sandalwood: Stress-reducing, sensuous

Spearmint: Refreshing, stimulating

Ylang-ylang: Uplifting, sensuous

FOR WE ARE THE AROMA OF CHRIST TO
GOD AMONG THOSE WHO ARE BEING SAVED
AND AMONG THOSE WHO ARE PERISHING
2 CORINTHIANS 2:15

MORE WAYS TO *USE ESSENTIAL OILS IN WINTER:

1. **DIFFUSION:** USE AN ESSENTIAL OIL DIFFUSER TO FILL YOUR HOME WITH THE AROMA OF ESSENTIAL OILS. DIFFUSING OILS LIKE EUCALYPTUS, PEPPERMINT, AND TEA TREE CAN HELP CLEAR CONGESTION AND IMPROVE RESPIRATORY HEALTH.
2. **INHALATION:** ADD A FEW DROPS OF ESSENTIAL OIL TO A BOWL OF STEAMING WATER AND INHALE THE STEAM TO HELP RELIEVE NASAL CONGESTION AND COLD SYMPTOMS.
3. **TOPICAL APPLICATION:** DILUTE ESSENTIAL OILS WITH A CARRIER OIL AND APPLY TO THE SKIN FOR SOOTHING RELIEF. OILS LIKE LAVENDER, CHAMOMILE, AND ROSEMARY CAN HELP WITH RELAXATION AND PROMOTE A SENSE OF WELL-BEING DURING THE WINTER MONTHS.
4. **HOT COMPRESS:** ADD A FEW DROPS OF ESSENTIAL OIL TO A WARM COMPRESS AND APPLY TO ACHY MUSCLES OR JOINTS FOR SOOTHING RELIEF.

*REMEMBER TO ALWAYS DILLUTE ESSENTIAL OILS PROPERLY AND PERFORM A PATCH TEST BEFORE USING THEM ON YOUR SKIN. CONSULT WITH A HEALTHCARE PROFESSIONAL OR AROMATHERAPIST IF YOU HAVE ANY SPECIFIC HEALTH CONCERNS OR QUESTIONS ABOUT USING ESSENTIAL OILS IN WINTER.

WE'RE CALLED TO RELY ON HIM

"Trust in the Lord completely, and do not rely on your own opinions. With all your heart, rely on Him to guide you, and He will lead you in every decision you make."

What would life look like if we stopped stressing and started dreaming? If we let go of our worries and fully embrace the dreams God has placed in our hearts? This verse invites us into a life of complete trust—a life where we don't have to figure it all out on our own.

I'll be the first to admit that trusting the Lord completely is easier said than done. For years, i perfected the art of worrying. I always had a plan B ready, just in case God didn't come through. Looking back, it's almost funny—almost. At the time, it was exhausting. All that worrying and overthinking drained me, and eventually, it led to burnout.

The beauty of this verse lies in its simplicity: we're called to rely on Him, not on ourselves. The Passion Translation paints this so vividly—we don't have to rely on our limited wisdom when we have access to heavenly intelligence! God's guidance is perfect, and it's always available. Isn't that exciting?

I'll never forget a moment when this truth came alive for me. I was at the end of my rope, utterly overwhelmed by setbacks and problems i couldn't solve. My mind was racing with opinions, strategies, and what-ifs. I felt like a one-person think tank running on fumes.

DREAM EVEN BIGGER WITH HIM

Then, in a rare moment of quiet, I paused to spend time with God. In the stillness, I sensed Him saying,
"Now, if you're done moping around, I'd like to show you something."

The humor in His tone caught me off guard, and I burst out laughing. In that instant, the heavy atmosphere lifted, and my worries disappeared. I realized that all my striving and stressing was unnecessary. God already had the answers I was desperately searching for.

January is a season brimming with fresh starts, blank calendars, and the excitement of new possibilities. It's the perfect time to pause, reflect, and dream with God. Why? Because dreaming with God is about more than setting goals or making resolutions—it's about aligning our hearts with His and envisioning the future He has in store for us.

God is a God of vision. From the creation of the world to the intricate plans He has for each of us, His heart overflows with dreams for His children. And He's already placed seeds of those dreams in your heart—passions, ideas, and desires that reflect His purpose for your life. This month, why not take some intentional time to nurture those dreams and dream even bigger with Him?

Sofia

Dream
VISUALIZE THE DREAMS GOD
HAS PLACED ON YOUR HEART

CREATE A VISION BOARD

A vision board is a powerful tool to help you articulate and visualize the dreams God has placed in your heart. It's not just about cutting out pretty pictures or inspiring quotes; it's about prayerfully asking God what He wants to birth in your life this year.

- **Set The Atmosphere:** Begin by spending time in prayer. Ask God to show you His dreams for your life and to give you clarity and boldness as you create your vision board.
- **Gather Your Materials:** Find magazines, printed images, or even draw your ideas. Include scriptures that inspire you, words that capture your dreams, and images that reflect what you feel God is calling you toward.
- **Dream Boldly:** Don't be afraid to think big! What dreams have you dismissed as "too much" or "impossible"? Remember, God's plans are often far bigger than what we could ever imagine.

When you have assembled your vision board and are happy with it - the best part - take action! The power of a vision board lies in its ability to continuously inspire and motivate you towards reaching your goals. Keep it someplace where you see it daily, and pray about the next action steps. God is faithful, and He will see to it that what He has promised will come through. Rich blessings!

COOKING IS LOVE
MADE VISIBLE

CHICKEN SOUP

I LOVE TO MAKE SOUPS IN THE WINTER. CHOPPING THE INGREDIENTS TO THIS SOUP IS ALMOST A MEDITATIVE ACT, AND THE FRESH AROMA THAT FILLS THE KITCHEN IS SO DELICIOUS. THIS SOUP IS THE ONE MY CHILDREN USED TO LOVE WHEN THEY WERE LITTLE. THIS VERSION IS REALLY GOOD AND ENJOYED WITH FRESH BREAD AND SOME HERBS.

YOU WILL NEED:

- 1 POUND CHICKEN OF CHOICE CUBED
- 2 TBS BUTTER / OLIVE OIL
- 2 LARGE CARROTS, CHOPPED
- 1 LARGE ONION, CHOPPED
- 4 GLOVES GARLIC, CHOPPED
- 2 STALKS OF CELERY, CHOPPED
- FRESH HERBS
- 2 BAY LEAVES
- 1 CUP OF FROZEN SWEET CORN
- 8-9 CUPS OF HIGH-QUALITY CHICKEN BROTH
- SALT AND PEPPER TO TASTE

JUST IN CASE YOU WANT A VARIATION, YES, CHICKEN NOODLES:

- 5 OUNCES EGG NOODLES OR PASTA OF CHOICE
- SMALL CAN OF COCONUT MILK

TASTE LIKE SUMMER

HERE IS HOW TO DO IT:

I ALWAYS START WITH MELTING THE BUTTER IN A FRYING PAN. WHEN THE BUTTER HAS MELTED, ADD ONIONS, GARLIC, AND CELERY AND SAUTÉ FOR A FEW MINUTES; ADD THE CARROTS AND STIR EVERY FEW MINUTES UNTIL THEY START SOFTENING. WHEN THEY LOOK PERFECT, REMOVE THEM TO A LARGE POT OVER MEDIUM HEAT. ADD BAY LEAVES AND HERBS ON TOP. ADD THE CHICKEN BROTH AND BRING THE POT TO A LOW SIMMER.

ADD SOME FRESH BUTTER TO THE FRYING PAN AGAIN AND BRIEFLY FRY THE CHICKEN CUBES - THEY DON'T HAVE TO BE PERFECTLY COOKED BECAUSE THEY WILL SIMMER IN THE SOUP STOCK - THIS IS ONLY TO GIVE THEM SOME COLOR AND TO ADD TEXTURE. WHEN DONE, ADD THESE TO THE POT. ADD SOME WATER TO THE FRYING PAN TO COLLECT THE DELICIOUS FLAVORS LEFT BEHIND FROM FRYING THE VEGETABLES AND CHICKEN, AND ADD TO THE POT.

LET THE SOUP SIMMER FOR 15 - 25 MINUTES; DON'T BE IN A HURRY. LET THE FLAVORS DEVELOP. REMOVE BAY LEAVES, ADD SALT AND PEPPER TO TASTE. TAKE THE POT OUT AND ADD THE FROZEN CORN AND SOME FRESH HERBS ON TOP. LET SIT FOR A FEW MINUTES BEFORE SERVING. THE CORN SHOULD BE WARM AND TASTE LIKE SUMMER.

Pray
MAY MY PRAYER BE SET BEFORE
YOU LIKE INCENSE;
MAY THE LIFTING UP OF MY
HANDS BE LIKE THE EVENING
SACRIFICE!
PSALMS 141:2

"Pour out all your worries and stress upon him and leave them there, for he always tenderly cares for you" 1 Peter 5:7

It never ceases to amaze me how intimately God knows us. He understands our tendencies to worry and stress, and He knows how difficult it can be for us to truly let go. Even when we bring our burdens to Him in prayer, it's all too easy to pick them up again as soon as we leave our prayer closet.

Life is full of uncertainties and challenges, and it's so natural to feel overwhelmed. Stress and anxiety often creep in before we even realize it. Yet, how often do we forget that these burdens don't belong to us in the first place? God didn't create us to carry them alone.

What an incredible truth it is to know that we can leave all of our worries and stress at the feet of Jesus. He doesn't just hear us—He tenderly cares for us. This isn't a passive kind of care; it's active, intentional, and deeply personal. The same God who holds the universe in his hands invites us to release everything to Him, trusting that He will carry it for us.

I've developed a morning habit that has become a source of great peace in my life: early hours spent in prayer, just me, Jesus, and a cup of coffee. It's during these moments of quiet reflection that I pour out my heart to Him—the good, the bad, and the downright messy. And every time, without fail, I am met with His peace, a peace that surpasses understanding.

TRUST FIRST

This peace doesn't always change my circumstances, but it changes me. It reminds me that I don't have to face life's challenges alone. I know that I am seen, heard, and cared for by a God who is infinitely loving.

What I've discovered is that trusting God often requires taking leaps of faith. It's not enough to simply hear His promises—we need to actively apply them to our specific situations. The bigger the problem, the more time I find myself needing to regain perspective. Worries and stress can easily cloud my thinking, making it difficult to apply God's word to my circumstances—to have faith and to truly trust in His promises.

I think this is one of the most important lessons we need to learn. Instead of insisting on understanding first and trusting second, we need to trust first—to take God's words as the ultimate truth. If He says He will always tenderly care for us, then that is what we can trust to happen, no matter what things look or feel like right now.

If you're holding on to stress or worry today, let this verse remind you of the invitation Jesus extends to you. Pour it all out to Him—every fear, every concern—and trust that He is strong enough to carry it and tender enough to care for your heart. And once you leave it with Him, resist the urge to pick it back up. He's got you, and He always will.

So, take a moment, let go of your burdens, and receive His tender care.

Sofia

CINNAMON COFFEE SMOOTHIE

INGREDIENTS

1 LARGE BANANA, SLICED AND FROZEN
1 CUP VANILLA-FLAVOR LOW-FAT GREEK YOGURT
2 TBSP. CINNAMON DOLCE SYRUP
1 TBSP. WHITE CHOCOLATE-FLAVOR SAUCE
1 TSP. VANILLA
¼ TO ½ TSP. INSTANT ESPRESSO COFFEE POWDER
¾ CUP ICE CUBES

DIRECTIONS

IN A BLENDER, COMBINE THE FIRST SEVEN INGREDIENTS (THROUGH ICE CUBES).

COVER AND BLEND UNTIL SMOOTH. GARNISH EACH SERVING WITH WHIPPED TOPPING AND/OR GROUND CINNAMON.

MAKES 2 SERVINGS (1 CUP EACH).

OPTIONAL GARNISH

REDDI - WHIP TOPPING
GROUND CINNAMON

EVERYONE LOVES COFFEE, RIGHT?

FOR SOME, THE LOVE FOR COFFEE IS SO DEEP THAT THEY WISH TO SET UP A COFFEE IV DRIP SYSTEM NEXT TO THEIR BED FOR A CONTINUOUS CAFFEINE INFUSION, BUT LET'S BE REAL, THIS MIGHT BE TAKING ITS DEVOTION A TAD TOO FAR. WHILE 90% OF AMERICANS START THEIR DAY WITH A CUP, ANOTHER 70% NEED A SECOND OR THIRD CUP THROUGHOUT THE DAY TO KEEP THEM GOING. THESE STATISTICS WERE 100% MADE UP BY ME, BUT YOU GET THE POINT, RIGHT?

THERE ARE MANY OF US WITH A COFFEE ADDICTION THAT PLAYS A KEY ROLE IN OUR DAILY LIVES. PERSONALLY, I DRINK COFFEE EVERY MORNING, AND ON A DAY I DON'T, MY MIND GOES WILD. MY BLOOD TYPE IS PROBABLY A BLEND OF COLOMBIAN AND ETHIOPIAN ROAST.

JUST IMAGINE WHEN GOD WILL GRANT ALL THE DESIRES OF YOUR HEART, AND COFFEE IS ONE OF THEM. WHAT WOULD IT BE LIKE? MAYBE A TOWN WHERE THE AROMA OF COFFEE WAFTED THROUGH THE AIR LIKE A COZY BLANKET, A MAGICAL PORTAL THAT TRANSPORTED US TO A REALM WHERE EVERYTHING WOULD BE MADE OF COFFEE BEANS. PICTURE RIVERS FLOWING WITH MOCHA, MOUNTAINS OF FROTHY LATTE FOAM, AND TREES DRIPPING WITH CARAMEL MACCHIATO. WE WOULDN'T BELIEVE OUR EYES - IT WOULD BE A CAFFEINE LOVER'S PARADISE!

BACK TO REALITY. YOU CAN STILL DREAM OF A COFFEE MUG THE SIZE OF A BATHTUB IN YOUR HANDS AND REMEMBER THAT GOD KNOWS EVERYTHING ABOUT YOU - YOUR THOUGHTS, DESIRES, TEMPTATIONS, AND HE WILL BE THERE TO SUPPLY YOU WITH THE BEST SOLUTIONS. FOREVER. JUST BELIEVE.

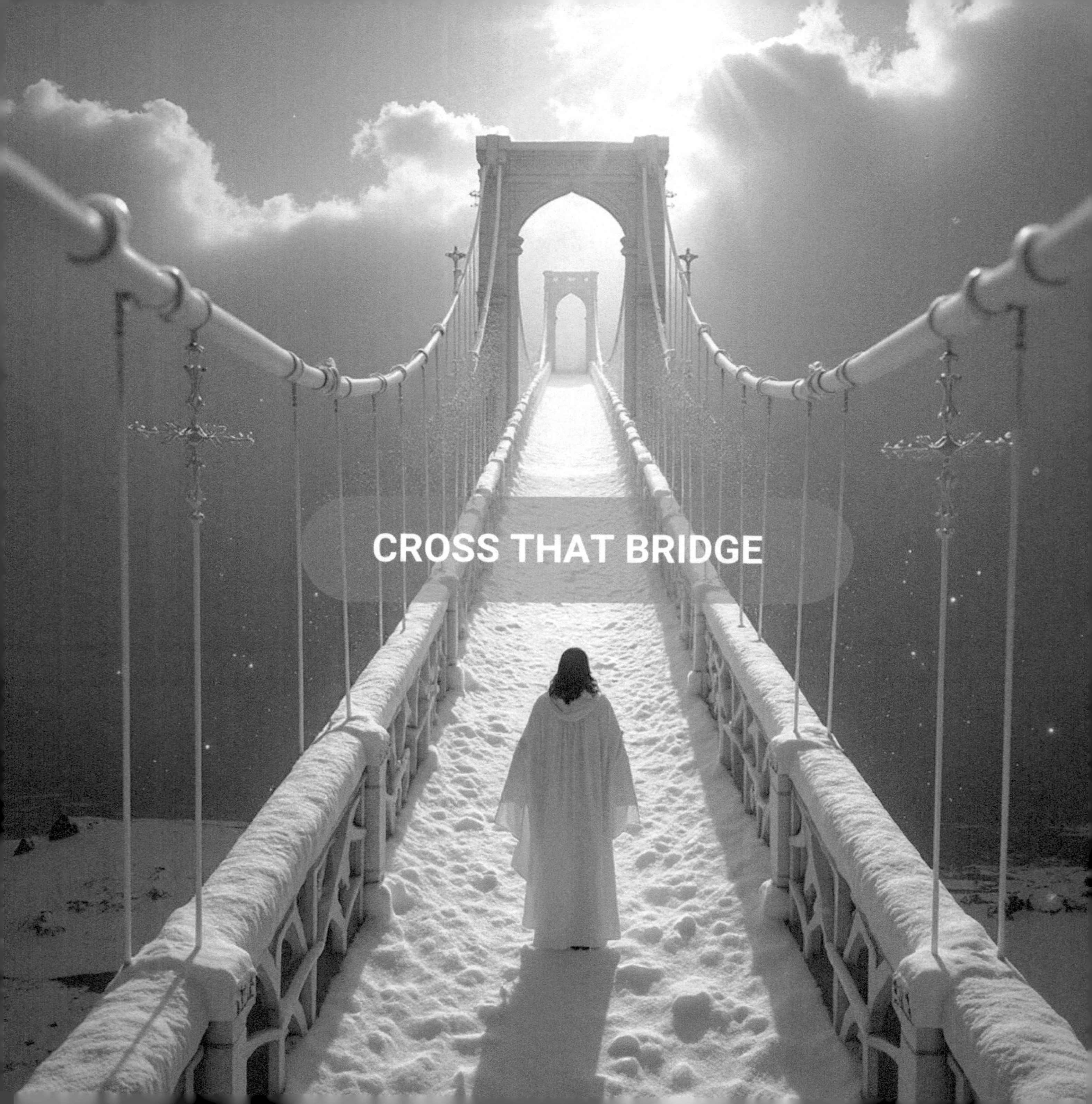
CROSS THAT BRIDGE

Life is like a journey with many important steps that help us reach our goals. Just as we need to see a nurse before a doctor, drive over a bridge to cross a mountain, or order from a waitress before enjoying a meal, we encounter necessary steps that connect us to our final goal or destination.

In Christianity, Jesus is seen as the crucial link to God. This concept is beautifully captured in john 14:6, where Jesus said, "I am the way and the truth and the life. No one comes to the Father except through me." Jesus is not only a bridge but a Savior who was sacrificed for our redemption.

Embracing Jesus as the bridge to heaven holds immeasurable importance in the life of a believer. Just as Jesus humbled Himself to the lowest point to secure our salvation, we, too, must humble ourselves before Him to receive the precious gift of eternal life. Jesus, who is fully divine yet became fully human, exemplifies the epitome of selfless love and sacrifice. Through His death on the cross, He shattered the barriers between humanity and heaven, paving the way for us to attain salvation and reconciliation with God.

By acknowledging Jesus as our Savior and following His teachings, we open our hearts to the infinite grace and mercy that flow from Him. He becomes our Advocate, our Intercessor, and our constant Companion in the journey towards heaven. With Him as our guide, we are empowered to overcome sin, navigate life's challenges, and ultimately find peace and fulfillment in the promise of eternal life.

May our lives be a testimony to the transformative power of having Jesus as our Savior, and may we find eternal joy and peace in His abiding presence, both now and in the heavenly realms to come.

Julia

GOD AND OXYGEN ARE BOTH INVISIBLE,
YET ESSENTIAL FOR LIFE

“It is better to take refuge in the Lord than to trust in man.”

I love using this small meditation when I am alone to unwind and remind myself how powerful our God is. Try it. Do it slowly. Close your eyes for a moment and take a deep breath. Now, do it again, even more slowly, and feel the air flow through your lungs. It feels so good!

We can’t live without oxygen. Pause and realize how blessed we are to have something so important and it’s free. Air. Just breathe.

We can stay alive for weeks without food. Without water, we can survive for several days, but without air, one cannot live for more than a few minutes.

Now, let's remember something. We don’t have any air; it was given to us by someone who made it and knows we need it. God!

Even science can’t argue with this global fact, although they figured out over the years how to make it in small amounts to sell it. If one wants to dive underwater, they have to buy oxygen to keep breathing. It costs approximately $40 to fill one tank, for something we can’t even see and was given to us free in the first place.

As we are breathing and appreciating every breath we take, let us give thanks to the One who provided it to us free of charge. Both of them, God and oxygen, are invisible, but we can’t survive a minute without one provided by the other.

Julia

BUILD A SNOW ANGEL

"GOD SAYS THAT ANGELS ARE MESSENGERS WHO SERVE AND PROTECT HIS PEOPLE," FROM HEBREWS 1:14. SO INSTEAD OF BUILDING A SNOWMAN, WHY NOT SCULPT A MAJESTIC ANGEL OUT OF SNOW? EMBRACE THE BEAUTY OF WINTER AND LET YOUR CREATIVITY SOAR LIKE THE ANGELS IN THE HEAVENS ABOVE. BUILDING A SNOW ANGEL CAN BE A FUN AND CREATIVE ACTIVITY, SO FEEL FREE TO ADD YOUR OWN PERSONAL TOUCHES. BUILD A SNOW ANGEL, EVEN IF YOU'RE ON A SANDY BEACH.

TO BUILD A SNOW ANGEL, FOLLOW THESE STEPS:

1. GATHER YOUR MATERIALS: SCARF AND MITTENS FOR DECORATION FIND A CLEAR, SNOW-COVERED AREA. IT'S BEST TO CHOOSE A SPOT WITH FRESH, UNDISTURBED SNOW. THE SNOW SHOULD BE STICKY AND PACKABLE SO IT STICKS TOGETHER EASILY.
2. LIE FLAT ON YOUR BACK IN THE SNOW.
3. STRETCH OUT YOUR ARMS AND LEGS, MAKING SURE TO LEAVE AN IMPRESSION IN THE SNOW.
4. CAREFULLY MOVE YOUR ARMS UP AND DOWN, CREATING THE "WINGS" OF THE SNOW ANGEL.
5. MOVE YOUR LEGS SLIGHTLY APART AND BACK TOGETHER TO CREATE THE "DRESS" OF THE SNOW ANGEL.
6. BE GENTLE AS YOU GET UP SO YOU DON'T RUIN THE DESIGN.
7. START BY FILLING THE MIDDLE SECTION OF THE "ANGEL" WITH THE SNOW TO FORM THE BASE. DRAW LARGE WINGS UNTIL IT'S THE DESIRED SIZE FOR THE BODY.
8. DRESS YOUR ANGEL WITH A SCARF AND MITTENS FOR A FINISHING TOUCH.

ADMIRE YOUR CREATION AND MAYBE TAKE SOME PHOTOS TO REMEMBER IT BY!

THERE IS PROFOUND
POWER IN THE PAUSE

In a world that glorifies busyness, pausing can feel unnatural, even unsettling. We're so accustomed to filling every moment with activity, every silence with sound, and every opportunity with action that the very idea of stopping feels counterproductive. Yet, there is profound power in the pause—a power we often overlook.

Pausing isn't about doing nothing; it's about creating space. It's in the stillness that we allow ourselves to reconnect with God, to realign our hearts, and to receive what we've been too busy to notice. When we pause, we open the door to something extraordinary: fresh vision, new insight, and the inner strength that grows in moments of quiet surrender.

Psalm 46:10 says,
"Be still, and know that I am God."

It's a simple command but one of the most challenging to obey. Stillness requires trust. It means letting go of the need to constantly strive and acknowledging that God is in control. In those moments of pause, we're reminded that we are not the ones holding the universe together—He is.

IT'S IN THE PAUSE THAT WE ARE
RENEWED, RESTORED,
AND READY TO STEP FORWARD

Even in our prayer lives, we can fall into the trap of constant activity. We plead, ask, and petition, pouring out our hearts to God, but how often do we simply sit in His presence? How often do we pause and listen? It's in these quiet moments that we often hear His gentle whisper, receive His guidance, and feel His peace washing over us.

Jesus himself modeled the power of the pause. Throughout His ministry, He frequently went to quiet places to pray and be with the Father. These moments of stillness didn't hinder His work; they empowered it. In the same way, pausing doesn't make us less productive—it equips us to be more intentional, more aligned with God's will, and more attuned to His voice.

When we take time to pause and contemplate the goodness and kindness of God, something shifts within us. Our perspective changes. The chaos of life fades into the background, and we're reminded of the bigger picture: God's unchanging love and faithfulness. In the stillness, we find clarity and strength to face whatever lies ahead.

So, let's dare to embrace the pause. Let's create moments of quiet in our day to simply rest in God's presence, to be still and know. In doing so, we'll discover that the pause isn't empty—it's filled with power. It's in the pause that we are renewed, restored, and ready to step forward with fresh purpose and strength.

Sofia

THE MEATBALLS

MEATBALLS ARE THE GO-TO COMFORT FOOD IN OUR HOUSE. WHETHER YOU SERVE THEM WITH SPAGHETTI OR WITH SMASHED POTATOES DOESN'T REALLY MATTER; THEY ALWAYS TASTE WONDERFUL.

YOU WILL NEED:

- ROUGHLY 2 POUNDS OF GROUND BEEF
- 1 CUP SOUR CREAM / CRÈME FRAÎCHE
- 2 TEASPOONS DRIED HERBS
- 1/2 TEASPOON BLACK PEPPER
- 1/2 TEASPOON SPICE CUMIN (OPTIONAL)
- 1 TEASPOON FINE SEA SALT
- 1 TEASPOON GOOD QUALITY HONEY
- 3/4 CUP YELLOW ONION CHOPPED
- 4 CLOVES GARLIC, PRESSED OR MINCED
- 1 SMALL STALK OF CELERY, FINELY CHOPPED
- BUTTER
- 2-3 CANS OF GOOD QUALITY CRUSHED TOMATO
- 3 TABLESPOONS TOMATO PASTE

FEEL FREE TO EXPLORE WITH THE RECIPE. IT IS VERY RARE TO MAKE THESE MEATBALLS UNLIKABLE, AND A TINY VARIATION ONLY MAKES THEM MORE INTERESTING. IN MY DRIED HERBS MIX, THERE IS USUALLY THYME. PARSLEY AND OREGANO, BUT OTHER HERBS WORK WELL TOO. FEEL FREE TO EXPLORE!

HERE IS HOW TO DO IT:

PUT THE SOUR CREAM IN A BIG BOWL. ADD DRIED HERBS, SPICE CUMIN, BLACK PEPPER, SEA SALT AND HONEY. MIX THOROUGHLY AND LET SIT WHILE YOU GENTLY SAUTÉ THE FINELY CHOPPED ONIONS, GARLIC AND CELERY IN BUTTER. LET THE ONION MIXTURE COOL BEFORE ADDING IT TO THE SOUR CREAM MIXTURE. MIX IN THE MEAT UNTIL THE MIXTURE IS EVEN AND THE SPICES ARE WELL DISTRIBUTED. LET THE MIXTURE REST IN THE REFRIGERATOR BEFORE FORMING THE MEATBALLS. HEAT THE OVEN TO 425°F AND LINE A LARGE RIMMED BAKING SHEET WITH PARCHMENT PAPER.

USE A SPOON OR A COOKIE SCOOP TO MAKE EVEN SIZE PIECES. ROLL EACH PIECE GENEROUSLY WITH YOUR HANDS TO FORM EVEN BALLS. USE DISPOSABLE GLOVES OR DIP YOUR HANDS FREQUENTLY IN ICE-COLD WATER TO PREVENT STICKING. PLACE THE MEATBALLS ON THE BAKING SHEET AND BAKE UNTIL GOLDEN BROWN (10 - 15 MINUTES).

WHEN THE MEATBALLS ARE READY, POUR THEM INTO A LARGE OVEN-SAFE DISH (IF THERE IS LIQUID IN THE BAKING SHEET, USE THAT TOO). POUR 2-3 CANS OF CRUSHED TOMATOES MIXED WITH THE TOMATO PASTE (SEASONED WITH A PINCH OF SALT, PEPPER, AND A DASH OF DRIED HERBS, IF DESIRED) OVER THE MEATBALLS AND RETURN THE DISH BACK TO OVEN. YOU CAN LOWER THE TEMPERATURE TO 380F AND LET THE DISH SIMMER UNTIL THE SAUCE THICKENS AND BUBBLES GENTLY AROUND THE MEATBALLS.

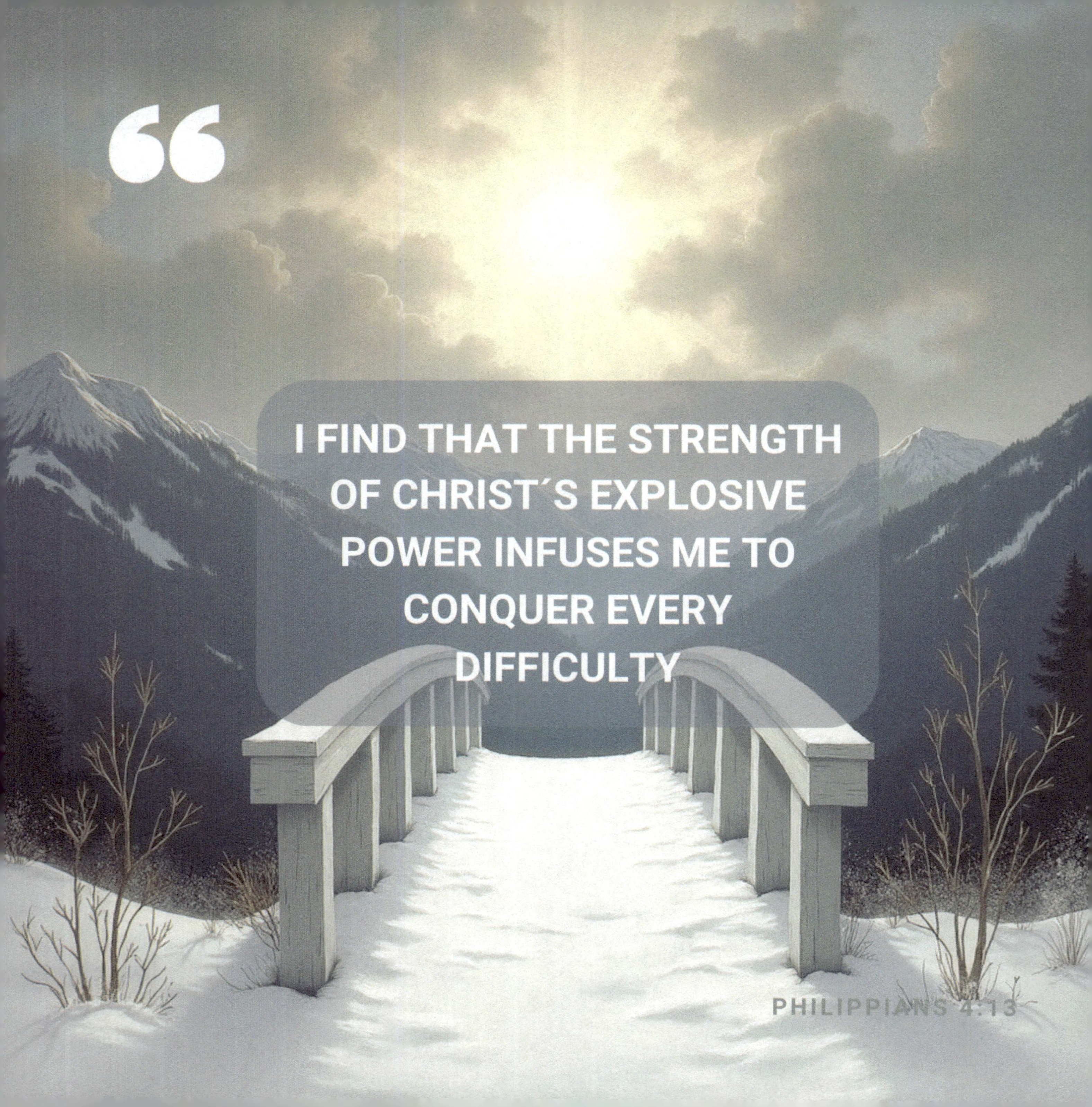
“
I FIND THAT THE STRENGTH OF CHRIST´S EXPLOSIVE POWER INFUSES ME TO CONQUER EVERY DIFFICULTY
PHILIPPIANS 4:13

Sometimes, we fall into the trap of believing that life should be easy, smooth, and free of challenges. Our culture often reinforces this idea with it's focus on convenience and instant gratification. Fast food, high-speed internet, and even fleeting relationships seem to echo the message that everything should come easily and quickly. But life doesn't work that way.

God, in His wisdom, understands the true nature of life—it's a journey filled with both beauty and hardship. It includes challenges, difficulties, and disappointments, as well as breathtaking moments of joy and wonder. Life is made up of valleys and mountain tops, and the contrast between the two helps us appreciate each experience fully. Without the struggles of the valleys, we wouldn't truly treasure the views from the peaks. Even psychologists tell us that challenges are essential for growth. When we embrace them without allowing bitterness to take root, we become stronger, more resilient, and better equipped for the journey ahead.

The beauty of this truth lies in the fact that it isn't about us—not our strength, not our abilities, and not even our expectations. It's about God—His sovereignty, His willingness, and His infinite ability to strengthen us in every moment.

I love how the Passion Translation puts it—it's often so vivid and relatable that it makes me smile or even laugh out loud. When I feel weak and weary, it reassures me that it's okay. Why? Because when I abide in Christ—when I lean on Him and find my refuge in Him—His strength becomes my strength. Like the Apostle Paul, I can learn to rejoice in my weaknesses. In those moments of vulnerability, Christ's power doesn't just meet me—it completely fills me.

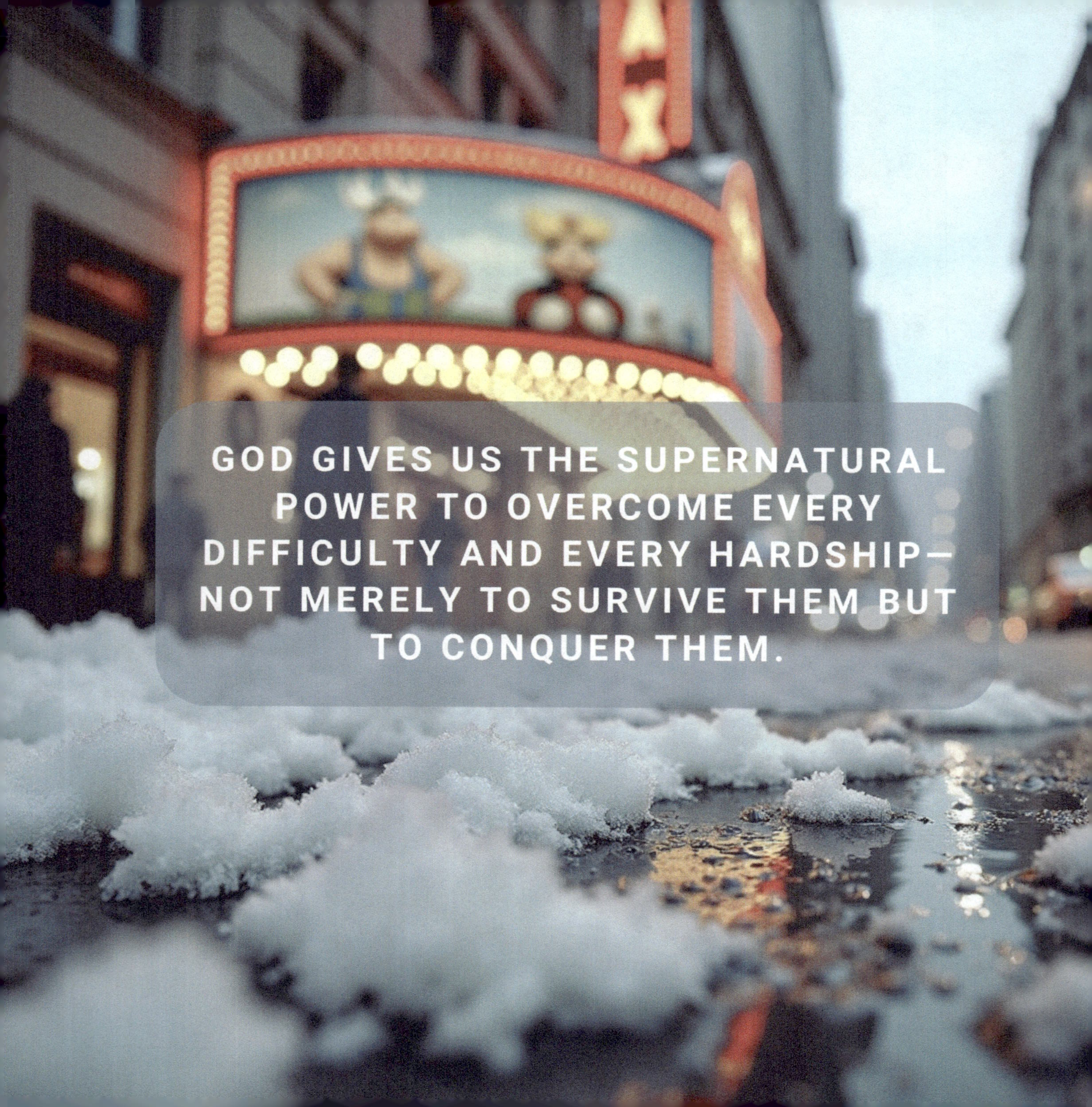
GOD GIVES US THE SUPERNATURAL
POWER TO OVERCOME EVERY
DIFFICULTY AND EVERY HARDSHIP—
NOT MERELY TO SURVIVE THEM BUT
TO CONQUER THEM.

And it's not just any kind of strength. It's Christ's explosive power. That phrase always brings to mind the cartoon characters Asterix and Obelix, particularly Asterix, who would drink the magic potion and suddenly have the strength to defeat entire armies. In a similar way, God gives us the supernatural power to overcome every difficulty and every hardship—not merely to survive them but to conquer them.

In my weakest moments, I've discovered a strength that is beyond anything I could muster on my own. It's His strength, alive and at work, in me, and it allows me to face life's challenges with hope and victory. Truly, in my weakness, I find His amazing, life-giving power!

Prayer: Lord, I'm in awe of Your unstoppable power! When life throws its hardest punches, and I feel weak and unworthy, remind me that Your strength is alive in me. You don't just help me survive the battle—You equip me to conquer it with explosive, unstoppable power! Let Your strength flood every corner of my heart and mind, turning my weakness into a stage for your glory. Thank You for making me more than a conqueror through Christ. I'm ready to face every challenge with You by my side, knowing victory is mine! In Jesus' mighty name, Amen!

Sofia

CHICKEN PUFF PASTRY

INGREDIENTS

4 CHICKEN TENDERLOINS
1/8 TEASPOON SALT
1/8 TEASPOON PEPPER
FLOUR, TO TASTE, FOR DUSTING A WORK SURFACE
1/2 (17.3-OUNCE, 2-COUNT) PACKAGE OF FROZEN PUFF PASTRY, THAWED, REMAINING PUFF PASTRY RESERVED FOR ANOTHER USE
1/2 CUP SPREADABLE SPINACH AND ARTICHOKE CREAM CHEESE
4 SLICES MUENSTER CHEESE, HALVED
1 EGG
1 TABLESPOON WATER

DIRECTIONS

PREHEAT THE OVEN TO 400 DEGREES F.

SPRINKLE THE CHICKEN TENDERLOINS WITH THE SALT AND THE PEPPER. SET IT ASIDE.

USING THE FLOUR, LIGHTLY DUST A FLAT SURFACE, THEN ROLL OUT THE PUFF PASTRY INTO ABOUT A 14-INCH SQUARE.

CUT THE PUFF PASTRY INTO 4 SQUARES.

SPOON ABOUT 2 TABLESPOONS OF THE CREAM CHEESE INTO THE CENTER OF EACH OF THE PASTRY SQUARES.

TOP THE CREAM CHEESE ON EACH OF THE PASTRY SQUARES EVENLY WITH THE MUENSTER CHEESE AND THE CHICKEN TENDERLOINS.

MIX TOGETHER THE EGG AND THE WATER USING A WHISK.

LIGHTLY BRUSH OVER THE EDGES OF THE PUFF PASTRY WITH THE EGG MIXTURE.

BRING THE OPPOSITE CORNERS OF EACH OF THE PASTRY SQUARES OVER THE FILLING, PINCHING THE SEAMS TO SEAL THE POCKETS.

HE WILL YET FILL YOUR MOUTH
WITH LAUGHTER &
YOUR LIPS WITH SHOUTS OF JOY
JOB 8:21

PUT THE SEAM SIDE OF THE PASTRY DOWN ONTO A GREASED BAKING TRAY AND BRUSHED THE TOPS WITH THE REMAINING EGG MIXTURE.

BAKE THE PUFF PASTRIES UNTIL GOLDEN BROWN, ABOUT 18-22 MINUTES.

SERVE HOT!

BE CONTENT

Learning to be content, as expressed in Philippians 4:11-13 by the Apostle Paul, is a valuable lesson that transcends time and remains relevant in our modern lives. In a world filled with constant striving for more, contentment can be a rare and precious virtue. Paul's words remind us that true contentment does not come from external circumstances but rather from an inner attitude of satisfaction and peace. Contentment comes from the understanding of life rooted in Christ.

Contentment can be learned. It is a skill that requires practice and effort. It is not a passive state but an active choice that can be cultivated over time. Paul sets an example for us to follow, showing that contentment is attainable even in the face of challenges and hardships.

The key to finding contentment, according to Paul, lies in his faith in Christ. He asserts that he can do all things through Christ, who strengthens him, suggesting that his inner strength and contentment come from his relationship with God. By anchoring his contentment in his faith, Paul demonstrates that true and lasting contentment transcends the temporary ups and downs of life, providing a deeper sense of fulfillment and peace.

In every moment, seek the beauty of content in a spiritual world where joy is abundant and peace reigns supreme. We will only be truly content with what we have if we have Jesus.

Julia

FOCUS ONLY ON
POSITIVE EMOTIONS

HOW TO ACHIEVE CONTENTMENT:

- Write down the things you're grateful for (1 Thessalonians 5:18)
- Lay up for yourselves treasures in heaven (Matthew 6:19-21)
- Do not worry (Matthew 6:31-32)
- Pray more often (Philippians 4:6)
- Forgive
- Develop a habit to serve
- Focus on your blessings
- Get more sleep
- Read positive affirmations
- Stay true to your values
- Act kindly toward others
- Find joy in the small things
- Get rid of extra possessions (Luke 12:15)
- Take care of your spiritual and physical health
- Do things that make you peaceful
- Don't compare yourself to others
- Establish priorities
- Give more than you receive
- Trust God (Philippians 4:11-13)

Hebrews 13:5: Keep your lives free from the love of money and be content with what you have because God has said, "Never will I leave you; never will I forsake you."

YOU HAVE A PURPOSE

God tells us throughout the Bible that we are born to serve Him. We must love others and attend to their needs. Our purpose is to glorify God, teach and admonish one another in all wisdom, and with gratitude in our hearts, sing psalms... (Colossians 3:14)

Just as snowflakes are fragile and delicate, so too are the lives of individuals easily impacted by the challenges and trials of life. In James 1:2-4, we are reminded to **"Count it all joy, my brothers, when you meet trials of various kinds, for you know that the testing of your faith produces steadfastness. And let steadfastness have its full effect, that you may be perfect and complete, lacking in nothing."** As we navigate the struggles of life, going through storms, we must remember to dance like snowflakes in the wind, surrendering to the will of our Creator. In Psalm 30:11-12, we are encouraged, **"You have turned for me my mourning into dancing; you have loosed my sackcloth and clothed me with gladness, that my glory may sing your praise and not be silent."**

And when our time on earth comes to an end, like snowflakes melting back into the ground, we return to the Creator who created us. Ecclesiastes 12:7 reminds us: **"And the dust returns to the earth as it was, and the spirit returns to God who gave it."**

The essence of human life lies in loving others, serving, showing compassion, displaying kindness, and demonstrating a willingness to support those in need. Losing oneself to acts of kindness toward others is a powerful tool for self-realization.

Embrace the winter season as a time of reflection, renewal, purpose, and selfless service. May your heart be a vessel of boundless joy, overflowing with the divine purpose and blessings of a spiritual awakening. Let your soul dance to the rhythm of the universe, embracing the spiritual journey with a heart full of love, joy, and gratitude.

Julia

“
NOW MAY GOD, THE INSPIRATION AND FOUNTAIN OF HOPE, FILL YOU TO OVERFLOWING WITH UNCONTAINABLE JOY AND PERFECT PEACE AS YOU TRUST IN HIM
ROMANS 15:13

During my quiet times with the Lord, I love exploring different Bible translations and occasionally diving into commentaries for added depth. There's something wonderful about seeing the same verse expressed in different ways—it breathes new life into familiar words. One particular verse has become my go-to when I'm feeling down or simply need fresh inspiration.

"Now may God, the inspiration and fountain of hope, fill you to overflowing with uncontainable joy and perfect peace as you trust in Him. And may the power of the Holy Spirit continually surround your life with His super-abundance until you radiate with hope!"

I've discovered that when I sit with a Bible passage in silence, just letting it settle in my heart, God often reveals something. The last time I reflected on this verse, two words jumped out at me: overflowing and uncontainable. In a world so often marked by hardships and sorrow, how incredible is it that God offers us so much joy in His presence that it overflows? It's a joy so abundant, so uncontainable, that no matter how hard we try, we simply can't hold it all to ourselves.

And isn't that what we all truly long for—joy and perfect peace? The problem is that we often look for joy and peace in the wrong places. We chase after accomplishments, possessions, or relationships, thinking they will satisfy our souls. But the joy and peace we're seeking can only be found in God. He is the source, the fountain, and the sustainer of the very things our hearts crave.

GOD OFFERS US SO MUCH
JOY IN HIS PRESENCE
THAT IT IS SIMPLY
OVERFLOWING

So often, I fall into the trap of thinking I need to be the source. If only I tried harder, worked smarter, or did more, maybe I could muster up joy and peace on my own. But here's the thrilling truth: God is the fountain! Whenever we feel like something is missing—hope, joy, peace—we don't have to strive to produce it. We can simply come to Him, the Fountain of Hope, and drink deeply.

What's even more beautiful is that this overflow isn't just for us. The abundance God pours into our lives naturally spills over to others. It's such a simple yet profound process: as we trust God, He fills us with so much hope, joy, and peace that it runs over, blessing everyone around us.

For me, the hardest part is learning to stop striving and simply receive. But every time I let God's words sink from my head into my heart, everything shifts. Suddenly, I'm no longer trying to manufacture peace—I'm experiencing it. I'm no longer chasing after joy—it's bubbling up within me. God is my source, my superabundance, and He continuously fills me with His hope and joy.

So, if you're feeling weary, don't try to fix it all yourself. Instead, come to the Fountain. Let Him fill you until you're overflowing, and watch how that abundance transforms not only your life but also the lives of those around you.

Sofia

JUST AS PHYSICAL EXERCISE STRENGTHENS OUR MUSCLES, SO TOO DO THE TRIALS AND TRIBULATIONS WE FACE STRENGTHEN OUR SPIRITUAL MUSCLE

God allows challenges in our lives to strengthen our faith and maturity. Trials are like exercises for the soul, developing our spiritual strength and endurance.

In the realm of Christian faith, our strength is not measured by our ability to avoid problems but rather by our perseverance in the face of them. It is in times of trial and challenge that we are given the opportunity to grow and deepen our faith. Praise Him for every trial! In those moments of weakness, we can truly experience the power of God working in our lives.

We may not always understand God's reasons for allowing challenges and difficulties. He knows, and we are called to lean on Him for strength and guidance, trusting in His plan for us even when the path is unclear.

Remember, challenges are opportunities for growth and development. Embrace them with courage and faith. Surround yourself with fellow believers who can offer support, encouragement, and prayer during tough times. Sharing your struggles with others can provide comfort. Meditate on passages that remind you of God's love.

"Trust in the Lord with all your heart and lean not on your own understanding." Proverbs 3:5-6

Julia

CAN YOU SEE HIM?

Visualizing God's presence is a profound practice that can bring us closer to our Creator in a tangible way. Deuteronomy 31:8 reminds us.

"The LORD himself goes before you and will be with you; he will never leave you nor forsake you."

We can envision the lord holding us in His arms or standing in front of us. He did for Paul in the midst of His trials. This visualization not only provides comfort but also serves as a powerful reminder of God's constant presence in our lives.

As we go about our daily routines, it is essential to remember that God is always witnessing our actions and hearing our words. Just as the man refrained from using profanity in the presence of His pastor, we should also be mindful of our behavior in the presence of the Almighty. If we are hesitant to act a certain way in the sight of others, how much more should we be conscious of our actions in the presence of God, who is ever near?

Take time each day to visualize God's loving presence, to be mindful of our actions in His sight, and to draw near to Him. In doing so, we can nurture a deeper connection with our Creator and experience the peace and guidance that come from dwelling in His nearness.

Julia

FEBRUARY

CHAPTER 3

1 John 4:16
We know how much God loves us, and we have put our trust in his love.
God is love, and all who live in love live in God, and God lives in them.

“
CREATE IN ME A CLEAN
HEART OF GOD AND RENEW
A RIGHT SPIRIT WITHIN ME
PSALM 51:10

There's a deeply comforting truth that lies within these words: nothing in our lives is random. Every moment, every circumstance, every detail—no matter how small or seemingly insignificant—is part of a grand, purposeful plan that God is weaving together. It may be hard to grasp at times, but when we truly embrace this truth, it changes everything. It shifts the way we see life and the way we respond to its ups and downs.

So often, we find ourselves facing challenges—the unexpected detours, the struggles, the seasons of uncertainty—and we can't help but wonder, how could any good possibly come from this? We want answers. We crave meaning in the midst of hardship. But here's the beautiful promise: God is at work in all things for our good. He doesn't promise that life will be free of pain or obstacles, but He does promise that no matter what we go through, every trial, every joy, and every heartache is part of His perfect design. Nothing is wasted in God's kingdom. Every part of our story—good, bad, and everything in between—has a purpose in the grand narrative he is unfolding.

The key to finding peace in the midst of uncertainty is understanding that we are not aimlessly drifting through life. We are deeply loved by God, and we are part of His bigger purpose. This is the essence of what Paul writes in Romans 8:28. As His lovers—those called to walk in His love and fulfill His designed purpose—we are not just passive bystanders in the story of our lives. No, we are active participants and partners with God in the creation of something beautiful.

God is Love

To help visualize this, think about a tapestry for a moment. When you look at a tapestry up close, all you see are individual threads. Some of them are dark, some light. Some are twisted, others smooth. At first glance, it's hard to understand how these seemingly random threads can form anything meaningful. But when you step back and look at the entire tapestry from a distance, a stunning design emerges—a picture full of purpose, beauty, and intention. Our lives are much the same way. When we look at them closely, we may only see individual threads that don't seem to fit together. But from God's perfect vantage point, He sees the whole picture. He's the master weaver, and He's intentionally weaving every detail of our lives with love and purpose.

In the middle of our story, it's easy to get caught up in the moment and lose sight of the bigger picture. It's easy to get frustrated and lose hope. Luckily, we can trust God. He knows what He is doing, and nothing gets lost - He sees everything and knows everything. What a joy knowing that is!

Remember, your life has meaning. Every detail matters to God. He is working in you, through you, and for you, always bringing you closer to the perfect purpose He has designed for you. Even when you can't see it, trust that He is at work. The story He's writing for you is far grander than you can imagine, and every chapter is necessary to bring you into the fullness of His plans. Keep trusting. Keep walking. God is weaving your story with love, and He is faithful to bring it to completion.

Sofia

BUNS & HOT CHOCOLATE

THIS IS USUALLY THE BEST PART OF WINTER. A PERFECT TIME FOR LONG WALKS OUTSIDE, GOING SKIING AND SKATING ON THE LAKE. THE SUN IS GETTING BACK UP A BIT, AND THERE IS STILL PLENTY OF SNOW AND ICE TO ENJOY. THE SUN MAKES THE DIFFERENCE - SLOWLY BUT SURELY, THE DAYS ARE GETTING LONGER, AND YOU CAN FEEL THE HOPE ARISING. A PERFECT TIME TO ENJOY BUNS AND HOT CHOCOLATE OUT IN THE COLD.

WHAT YOU WILL NEED:

THE CINNAMON BUN RECIPE - THIS TIME, OMIT THE CINNAMON, SUGAR & BUTTER AND ROLL PLAIN BUNS INSTEAD. BAKE AND LET COOL.

FOR THE BACKPACK:

- THE BUNS, CUT IN HALF
- JAM (OPTIONAL)
- HEAVY WHIPPED CREAM IN A BOX / CAN
- HOT MILK IN A THERMOS FLASK
- COCOA, SUGAR, AND DARK CHOCOLATE
- CUPS AND SPOONS FOR THE CHOCOLATE

FIND A NICE LOCATION WITH A PERFECT VIEW. START WITH THE BUNS. FILL THE BUNS WITH JAM AND WHIPPED CREAM. IN EACH CUP, PLACE A GENEROUS CHUNK OF DARK CHOCOLATE, COCOA, AND SUGAR TO TASTE. POUR HOT MILK IN THE CUPS AND MIX GENTLY. TOP WITH SOME WHIPPED CREAM. ENJOY THE VIEW!

God's Way

Living life with faith is a thrilling journey, like driving a car without a map. So many roads to choose from, how do we know which one is the right one? We need GPS, the Global Positioning System which uses satellites to provide information to guide us.

Now replace the word “Global” with “God’s.” Now you have God’s Positioning System (GPS). Let Him guide you in the right direction. What’s good about this kind of GPS is you have 24-hour lifetime access without worrying about the WIFI output, speed limits, traffic jams, and being lost. You still have to learn how to navigate, but it will be worth the effort. Having the Bible as the main guide in your life will instruct you on how to live physically and spiritually safely and have guidance when you find yourself veering off the road. He who has mapped out the end from the beginning sees all routes, bumps, turns, and scenic views. Everyone can make their own decisions, but often, when doing so, we encounter crashes that sometimes could even be deadly. Driving with faith as our compass, we can navigate through the ups and downs of life and enjoy the view along the way.

By following God’s way, we can rest assured that our final destination will be simply the best in this life, and in our final city, the streets will be made of pure gold. Revelation 21:21: **"The great street of the city was of pure gold, like transparent glass."** Now, that’s the final destination worth driving toward, no matter the obstacles!

Julia

“
LET US APPROACH GOD'S THRONE OF GRACE WITH BOLDNESS
HEBREWS 4:16

What a remarkable invitation: to come before the Creator of the universe, the King of kings, with boldness. Hebrews 4:16 reminds us,

"Let us then approach God's throne of grace with confidence so that we may receive mercy and find grace to help us in our time of need."

This verse is both comforting and empowering. It invites us into a relationship with God that is intimate, personal, and unshakable.

In ancient times, approaching a king's throne was an act of great risk. Only those who were summoned, worthy, or in the king's favor dared come close. Yet, through Jesus, the dynamic has completely changed. The King Himself has thrown open the doors of HIS throne room and welcomes us to come near—not with fear or hesitation, but with boldness.

What gives us this boldness? It's not our own merit, achievements, or righteousness. It's the grace and sacrifice of Jesus. He has paved the way, tearing down every barrier that stood between us and God. Because of Him, we can approach confidently, knowing that we will be met with mercy and love, not judgment or rejection.

This boldness doesn't mean arrogance or entitlement. It's a humble boldness born of trust in His character. It's the boldness of a child running into their parent's arms, unafraid and assured of their love. Coming into the presence and staying in it for as long as you like, soaking in the heavenly atmosphere, tends to change everything.

Think about the power of this access. Whatever is going on in our lives, we don't have to navigate life alone. We have an open invitation to enter God's presence and lay everything at His feet. What a treasure that is! Whether it's our fears, biggest dreams, or failures, He meets us there with grace sufficient for every situation.

Imagine what your life would look like if you fully embraced this truth. What if, instead of hesitating or feeling unworthy, you stepped into His presence boldly every day? What if you made it a daily habit to spend time in the presence? What if you trusted Him enough to bring your biggest dreams, deepest struggles, and even your smallest concerns before Him?

This is the life we are called to—a life lived in close connection to God, where His grace empowers and strengthens us. So today, let us rise with confidence, approach His throne boldly, and experience the fullness of His love and grace.

Sofia

A cup of hot beverage can bring warmth and comfort to the soul. Whether it's a Cinnamon Dolce Latte or a strong peppermint tea, these drinks serve not only to satisfy our taste buds but also to invigorate our senses and provide a moment of respite from the chilly weather outside.

Just as a well-timed cup of coffee or tea can awaken the senses and provide a burst of energy, individuals who exhibit a strong sense of determination and zeal can have a significant impact on the world around them. Their fervor and commitment serve as a driving force for progress and transformation, inspiring others to take action and make a difference in their communities.

In contrast, lukewarm attitudes or beliefs that lack passion and energy may result in a sense of emptiness and unfulfillment. In the Revelation 3:15-16 He says, **"I know your deeds, that you are neither cold nor hot. I wish you were either one or the other! So, because you are lukewarm—neither hot nor cold—I am about to spit you out of my mouth."**

In this context, being "cold" refers to being completely against God and His teachings, while being "hot" means being passionately committed to following Him. Being "lukewarm" means being indifferent, apathetic, or half-hearted in one's faith or beliefs. God cherishes those who are passionate and on fire for Him, boldly proclaiming His truth and spreading His message of love and hope. Keep it hot!

Julia

TAKE A LONG
REFRESHING WALK IN
THE NATURE

TAKE A WALK IN THE FOREST*:

TAKING A WALK IN THE FOREST DURING THE WINTER IS ONE OF THE MOST UNDERESTIMATED REMEDIES FOR COMBATING THE WINTER BLUES, AND IT'S TRULY A HIDDEN GEM OF WELLNESS.

THE JAPANESE CALL IT FOREST BATHING, SHINRIN-YOKU. IT'S NOT ABOUT HIKING OR EXERCISING BUT ABOUT BEING PRESENT, SLOWING DOWN, AND CONNECTING WITH NATURE THROUGH ALL YOUR SENSES. THIS WAY OF BEING IN NATURE HAS MANY BENEFITS, BUT MOST OF ALL, IT GIVES YOU AN OPPORTUNITY TO FIND BALANCE AND SOMETHING AWE-INSPIRING.

- **CHOOSE THE RIGHT SETTING:** SELECT A PLACE WHERE YOU FEEL SAFE AND AT EASE.
- **UNPLUG:** LEAVE ALL DISTRACTIONS BEHIND.
- **ENGAGE YOUR SENSES:** NOTICE THE COLORS OF THE LEAVES, THE TEXTURE OF THE BARK, THE EARTHY SMELL OF MOSS, THE SOUNDS OF BIRDS, AND THE SENSATION OF THE BREEZE ON YOUR SKIN.
- **GO SLOWLY:** THERE'S NO RUSH. WALK AT A LEISURELY PACE, OR FIND A SPOT TO SIT AND SIMPLY TAKE IN YOUR SURROUNDINGS.

PRO TIP: TAKE A NICE SNACK ALONG. HOT SPICED TEA IS ALWAYS AN EXCELLENT CHOICE. SOME NUTS & RAISINS?

*SOME BENEFITS OF WALKING IN NATURE INCLUDE REDUCING STRESS AND ENHANCING RELAXATION, BOOSTING IMMUNE FUNCTION, IMPROVING MOOD AND MENTAL CLARITY, ENCOURAGING CREATIVITY AND PROBLEM-SOLVING, PROMOTING CONNECTION—TO NATURE, YOURSELF, AND GOD, SUPPORTING OVERALL PHYSICAL HEALTH, NATURAL LIGHT BOOSTS SEROTONIN.

UKRAINIAN BORSCHT

INGREDIENTS:

1 LB BEEF CHUCK, DICED
1 ONION, CHOPPED
4 MEDIUM BEETS, PEELED AND GRATED
2 CARROTS, PEELED AND GRATED
3 MEDIUM POTATOES, PEELED AND DICED
1/2 SMALL HEAD OF CABBAGE, SHREDDED
1 CAN (14 OZ) DICED TOMATOES
4 CUPS BEEF OR VEGETABLE BROTH
2 CLOVES OF GARLIC, MINCED
2 TBSP TOMATO PASTE
1 TBSP WHITE VINEGAR
2 BAY LEAVES
SALT AND PEPPER TO TASTE
SOUR CREAM AND FRESH DILL FOR SERVING

DIRECTIONS:

1. IN A LARGE POT, SAUTÉ THE BEEF CHUCK AND ONIONS UNTIL THE BEEF IS BROWNED AND THE ONIONS ARE SOFT.
2. ADD THE GRATED BEETS AND CARROTS TO THE POT AND COOK FOR ABOUT 5 MINUTES.
3. ADD THE DICED POTATOES, SHREDDED CABBAGE, DICED TOMATOES, BEEF BROTH, MINCED GARLIC, TOMATO PASTE, VINEGAR, AND BAY LEAVES TO THE POT. SEASON WITH SALT AND PEPPER.
4. BRING THE BORSCHT TO A BOIL, THEN REDUCE THE HEAT TO LOW AND LET IT SIMMER FOR ABOUT 45 MINUTES TO 1 HOUR, OR UNTIL ALL THE VEGETABLES ARE TENDER AND THE FLAVORS ARE WELL COMBINED.
5. ADJUST THE SEASONING WITH MORE SALT AND PEPPER IF NEEDED.
6. REMOVE THE BAY LEAVES BEFORE SERVING.
7. SERVE THE BORSCHT HOT WITH A DOLLOP OF SOUR CREAM AND A SPRINKLE OF FRESH DILL OR PARSLEY ON TOP.

ENJOY YOUR BORSH!

“
HE WHO DWELLS IN THE SHELTER
OF THE MOST HIGH WILL REST IN
THE SHADOW OF THE ALMIGHTY
PSALM 91:1

February is the month of love, but what kind of love? What if you feel unloved and betrayed, and your heart is broken?

Remember that you are not alone, and nothing is permanent. Time will numb and even heal those wounds that you might have. It might seem impossible to see or feel it at the moment, but trust in Him who heals and delivers - Jesus. He faced His own share of toxic relationships during His time on Earth. He encountered betrayal, rejection, and hostility from those around Him. Despite this, Jesus responded with love, compassion, and forgiveness. In Matthew 5:44, He instructs us to "Love your enemies and pray for those who persecute you." This powerful message reminds us that responding to toxicity with love and prayers. They will help transform the situation and protect our hearts from bitterness and resentment.

Just as winter brings bitter cold weather and gray cloudy days, toxic relationships can cast a shadow over our lives. However, just as the sun eventually breaks through the clouds and shines brightly, we too can emerge from the darkness of toxic relationships into the light of healing and wholeness. By looking to the example of Jesus Christ and drawing on the wisdom of the Bible, we can navigate these challenging relationships in a Godly manner.

Meanwhile, those of us who dwell in the shelter of the Most High will rest in the shadow of the Almighty by leaning on the power of prayer, forgiveness, and grace. We can bring light and love into our relationships, even those that may be challenging. Keep on loving in February and every day!

Julia

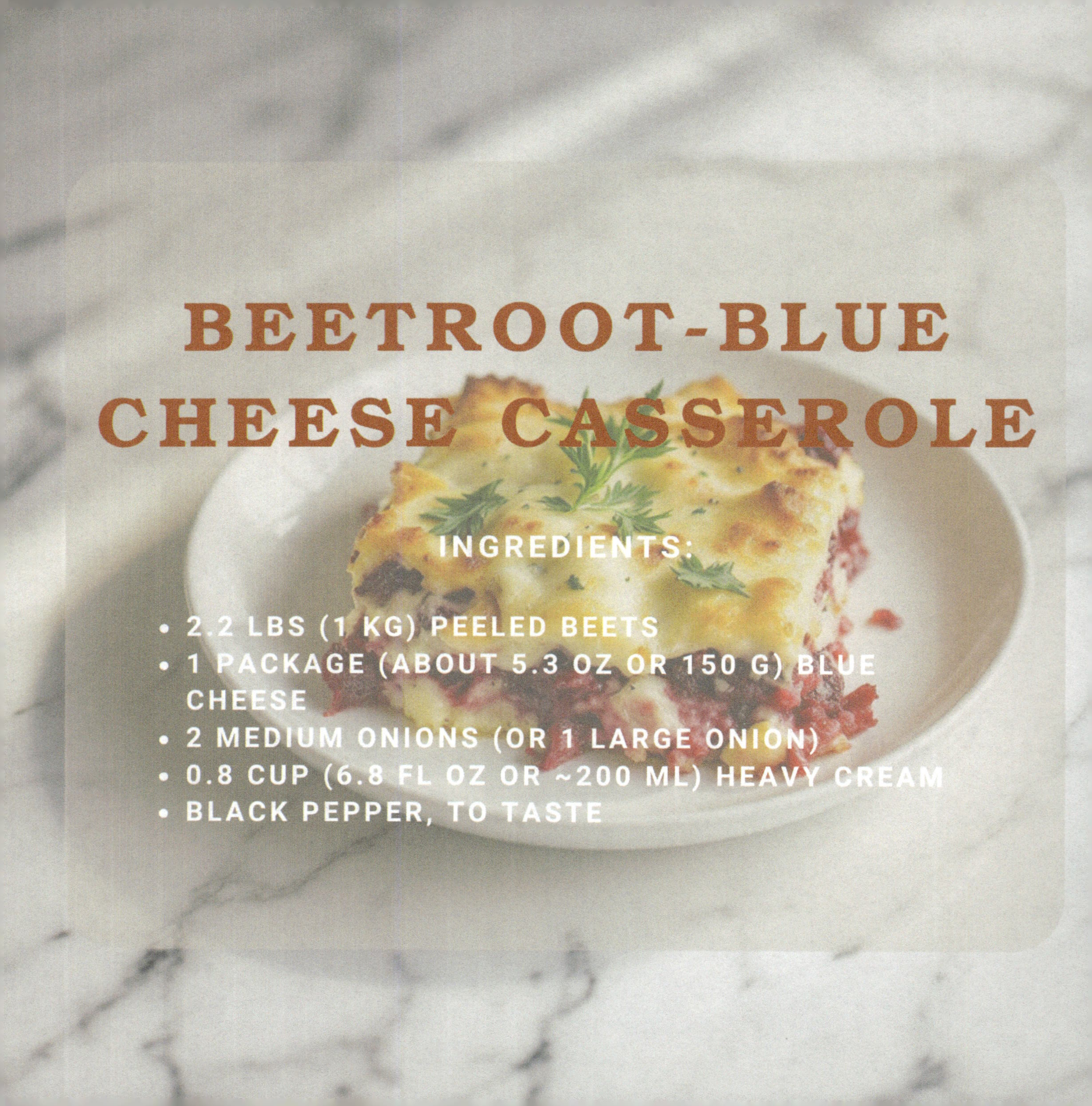

BEETROOT-BLUE CHEESE CASSEROLE

INGREDIENTS:

- 2.2 LBS (1 KG) PEELED BEETS
- 1 PACKAGE (ABOUT 5.3 OZ OR 150 G) BLUE CHEESE
- 2 MEDIUM ONIONS (OR 1 LARGE ONION)
- 0.8 CUP (6.8 FL OZ OR ~200 ML) HEAVY CREAM
- BLACK PEPPER, TO TASTE

INSTRUCTIONS:

- GRATE THE BEETS AND FINELY CHOP THE ONION.
- IN A BAKING DISH, LAYER THE GRATED BEETS, CHOPPED ONION, AND CRUMBLED BLUE CHEESE. SPRINKLE BLACK PEPPER BETWEEN THE LAYERS FOR FLAVOR.
- POUR THE HEAVY CREAM EVENLY OVER THE TOP OF THE LAYERS.
- BAKE AT 390°F (200°C) FOR APPROXIMATELY 1 HOUR.
- IF THE TOP BEGINS TO BROWN TOO MUCH, COVER THE DISH WITH ALUMINUM FOIL.

ENJOY THIS RICH, EARTHY CASSEROLE WITH SOME BREAD OR AS A SIDE DISH!

TRUST THE PROCESS

Throughout human history, the act of sharing a meal has been more than just a necessity for survival. It has been a deeply spiritual practice, one that fosters connection, gratitude, and joy. This sacred nature of hospitality finds its roots in scripture, where hosting and sharing food with others is often elevated to a divine act. One such profound reference comes from Hebrews 13:2: "Do not forget to entertain strangers, for by so doing some have unwittingly entertained angels." this verse speaks not only to the importance of kindness and generosity but also to the transcendent power of enjoying food in good company.

Sharing a meal is one of the simplest yet most profound expressions of hospitality. In the Gospels, Jesus frequently dines with others, using these occasions to teach, heal, and build relationships. From the wedding feast at Cana to the Last Supper, the act of breaking bread together is imbued with spiritual significance. These moments demonstrate that food is more than sustenance; it is a conduit for joy, love, and community.

When we share food with others, we partake in a timeless ritual that transcends cultural and temporal boundaries. Meals provide a setting for laughter, storytelling, and the exchange of ideas. They invite us to slow down, to savor not just the flavors on our plates but the presence of those around us.

By opening our homes and our hearts, we create opportunities for divine encounters and deepen our relationships with others. In the act of sharing food and fellowship, we honor the sacredness of life and the presence of the divine in our midst.

Sofia

THE SMALLEST OF
THINGS CAN HOLD THE
GREATEST OF POWERS

When life's trials weigh heavy on your heart,
And you feel completely torn apart,
Know that in those tests, sharp as a knife
There's a hidden purpose for your life.

God's hands are skilled, His plans divine,
Crafting you by His design,
To be a beacon shining bright,
In the darkness of the night.

With each lesson and each test,
He's molding you to be your best,
And when it seems too much to bear
He cradles you with utmost care.

So, trust the process and believe,
That in His time, you will perceive,
The masterpiece that you'll become,
Shaped by God, the Holy One!

Julia

SHE HAS NO FEAR OF WINTER
FOR HER HOUSEHOLD, FOR
EVERYONE HAS WARM
CLOTHES. SHE MAKES HER OWN
BEDSPREADS. SHE DRESSES IN
FINE LINEN AND PURPLE GOWNS
PROVERBS 31:21-31

The Heart beats tirelessly. This tiny but resilient organ, no larger than a fist, beat tirelessly day and night to keep its keeper alive.

With every pulsation, the heart whispers secrets of life and love, pumping life-giving blood to every corner of the body. Through valleys of veins and hills of arteries, the heart races on, a determined little hero in a never-ending quest for survival. It is not just the physical organ that pumps blood in our bodies, but it encompasses our entire being - our thoughts, emotions, desires, and intentions.

In the Christian faith, the concept of the heart holds great significance. Think about it. God is more concerned about your heart than he is about what you do. King Amaziah is noted for having a negative condition of the heart. (2 Chronicles 25:2). He did all the right things, but His heart was not right. Therefore, God was not pleased with him. That's a scary thing. We can do the right thing and yet have it not be acceptable to God because we do it with a wrong heart attitude. He delights in those who seek Him with sincerity and truth. Cherish it, nurture it, and let it guide you on your journey through life. In times when we feel like our emotions, desires, and feelings are overwhelming, take a moment to breathe and pray. Trust in your own resilience, and remember that you are capable of handling whatever comes your way.

Julia

CLASSIC UKRAINIAN CREPES (NALISNIKI)

INGREDIENTS:

- 1 CUP ALL-PURPOSE FLOUR
- 2 EGGS
- 1 1/2 CUPS MILK
- 2 TBSP SUGAR
- PINCH OF SALT
- BUTTER OR OIL FOR FRYING

INSTRUCTIONS:

1. IN A MIXING BOWL, WHISK TOGETHER THE FLOUR, EGGS, MILK, SUGAR, AND SALT UNTIL SMOOTH.
2. HEAT A NON-STICK SKILLET OVER MEDIUM HEAT AND LIGHTLY GREASE WITH BUTTER OR OIL.
3. POUR A SMALL LADLEFUL OF THE BATTER INTO THE SKILLET, SWIRLING IT AROUND TO SPREAD THE BATTER EVENLY.
4. COOK THE CREPE FOR ABOUT 2 MINUTES UNTIL THE EDGES START TO LIGHTLY BROWN, THEN FLIP AND COOK FOR ANOTHER MINUTE ON THE OTHER SIDE.
5. CONTINUE WITH THE REST OF THE BATTER, STACKING THE COOKED CREPES ON A PLATE.
6. SERVE WARM WITH YOUR FAVORITE FILLING, SUCH AS CARAMEL SOUSE, BANANAS, SWEET JAM, FRESH BERRIES, OR SAVORY FILLINGS LIKE CHEESE AND HAM.

TAKE HEART &
SAY A PRAYER

Dear God,

Today, I come to you with a humble heart, seeking your guidance and presence in my life. I ask that you create in me a pure heart, free from impurities and distractions that may lead me astray from your path. Help me to align my thoughts, words, and actions with your will so that I may walk in righteousness and bring glory to your name.

Renew a steadfast spirit within me, Lord, that I may stand firm in my faith and not be swayed by the challenges and temptations of this world. Grant me the strength and courage to follow you wholeheartedly, trusting in your unfailing love and wisdom to lead me on the right path.

May my heart be a reflection of your grace and mercy, overflowing with compassion, forgiveness, and kindness towards others. Let your light shine through me, touching the lives of those around me and drawing them closer to you.

I thank you, Lord, for your faithfulness and for the promise of transformation through your power. Guide me, mold me, and shape me into the person you created me to be, with a pure heart and a steadfast spirit devoted to serving you.

IN JESUS NAME, AMEN

Julia

“
AS LONG AS THE EARTH REMAINS, THERE WILL BE PLANTING AND HARVEST, COLD AND HEAT, SUMMER AND WINTER, DAY AND NIGHT
GENESIS 8:22

In this verse from Genesis, following the narrative of Noah's Ark and the great flood, we encounter one of the most profound assurances of God's faithfulness—His promise that the cycles of nature will endure. This declaration is more than a statement about the seasons; it's a pledge that speaks to the very heart of God's reliability and unchanging nature.

Winter, as part of this eternal rhythm, serves as a striking reminder of God's steadfastness. In the stillness and quiet of the season, when the world seems cold and lifeless, we are invited to reflect on the enduring consistency of God's commitments. No matter how bleak things may appear, just as winter is always followed by spring, so too are we assured that His plans for renewal and restoration will unfold in due time.

Life often mirrors the seasons. We all face winters of the soul—times of hardship, loss, or waiting. These moments can feel isolating and challenging, yet they carry a divine purpose. Winter, in its quiet way, prepares the earth for new growth. Beneath the frost-covered ground, seeds lie dormant, gathering strength to bloom when the time is right. In the same way, God is often at work in the unseen areas of our lives during these seasons of stillness and waiting.

love

By embracing the cold and darkness of winter, we find solace in the knowledge that it, too, plays an essential role in the grand design of life. Winter teaches us patience, resilience, and the beauty of slowing down to trust in God's timing. Just as the earth remains steadfast through the rhythms of seedtime and harvest, cold and heat, summer and winter, day and night, we can anchor our hearts in the faithfulness of our Creator.

Each cycle is a reminder that nothing is wasted. The hardships of winter pave the way for the joys of spring. The frozen ground will eventually give way to blossoming fields. This rhythm reflects God's promise not only for the earth but for our lives as well. As we trust in His unchanging nature, we find hope in the promise of brighter days ahead, strengthened by the assurance that He is always working for our good.

So, let us embrace this season with hearts full of gratitude. In the stillness, let us look for the beauty hidden in the frost and the lessons woven into the chill. Winter may feel like a time of waiting, but it is also a time of promise—a time to rest in the rhythm of God's faithfulness and anticipate the bountiful future he has planned for us.

Julia

“

THE LORD INSTRUCTS, “WRITE ALL THE WORDS THAT I HAVE SPOKEN TO YOU IN A BOOK.” THIS SIGNIFIES A DIVINE COMMITMENT TO RESTORATION, ENSURING THAT THESE PROMISES ARE NOT FORGOTTEN

JEREMIAH 30:2

WRITE A LETTER TO GOD

Overall, writing down your letters and what you want to communicate is a valuable practice. Writing a letter or a prayer to God can be a beautiful way to express your thoughts and feelings. In Deuteronomy 17:18-20, a king is instructed to personally transcribe God's word to deepen His reverence for the Lord. The act of writing down information enhances our likelihood of retaining it. Take a moment to reflect on your emotions and experiences, and let your words flow onto the page.

Your letter or prayer doesn't have to be perfect. What matters is the sincerity and honesty behind your words.

Trust that God is always listening, and your words will be received with love and understanding. Use this opportunity to pour out your heart, seek guidance, or simply express gratitude.

Allow yourself to be vulnerable and open in your communication with God. He is there to comfort and guide you. Remember that writing can be a therapeutic and cathartic process. Let your pen be your voice.

More benefits of writing down letters & prayers:

Clarity. Note prayer timings. Pass on to children. Track ANSWERED prayers AND life growth. Aid focus during prayers.

Ultimately, the act of writing a letter to God filled with love, gratitude, and a request for forgiveness can be a cathartic and transformative experience.

COMMIT TO THE LORD WHATEVER YOU DO, AND HE WILL ESTABLISH YOUR PLANS
PROVERBS 16:3

STEPS TO WRITE YOUR LETTER TO GOD:

FIND A QUIET SPACE, LIGHT A CANDLE, AND CREATE A PEACEFUL ATMOSPHERE TO ENHANCE YOUR CONNECTION WITH GOD. LET YOUR FAITH AND HOPE SHINE THROUGH YOUR WORDS AS YOU REACH OUT TO THE DIVINE. YOUR LETTER OR PRAYER CAN SERVE AS A POWERFUL REMINDER OF YOUR RELATIONSHIP WITH GOD AND THE STRENGTH OF YOUR FAITH.

1. **START WITH A PRAYER:** APPROACH THIS TASK WITH AN OPEN HEART AND MIND. TAKE A FEW MINUTES TO PRAY. THANK HIM FOR THE BLESSINGS, LOVE, AND POSITIVE EXPERIENCES IN YOUR LIFE. ASK HIM TO GUIDE YOU AND FILL YOU WITH HIS HOLY SPIRIT.
2. **WRITE FROM THE HEART:** WRITE THE LETTER AUTHENTICALLY, POURING OUT YOUR EMOTIONS, THOUGHTS, AND INTENTIONS IN A HEARTFELT MANNER. REMIND YOURSELF THAT HONESTY AND SINCERITY ARE KEY TO COMMUNICATING WITH GOD.
3. **SELF-REFLECTION AND ACCEPTANCE:** TAKE SOME TIME FOR SELF-REFLECTION AND ACKNOWLEDGE YOUR MISTAKES OR SHORTCOMINGS. EMPHASIZE THE IMPORTANCE OF SELF-ACCEPTANCE AND FORGIVENESS AS A FIRST STEP TOWARDS SEEKING FORGIVENESS FROM GOD.
4. **CULTIVATE A HEART OF LOVE AND GRATITUDE:** FOCUS ON THE LOVE AND BLESSINGS YOU HAVE RECEIVED FROM GOD AND EXPRESS GRATITUDE FOR THESE IN THE LETTER. BY EXPRESSING GRATITUDE, YOU CAN HELP SHIFT YOUR PERSPECTIVE AND FOSTER A SENSE OF CONNECTION WITH THE DIVINE.

REMINDER OF YOUR FAITH &
CONNECTION TO GOD

5. **SEEK FORGIVENESS WITH HUMILITY:** HUMBLY ASK FOR FORGIVENESS FOR YOUR SINS, SHOWING GENUINE REMORSE AND A WILLINGNESS TO CHANGE. REMIND YOURSELF THAT GOD'S MERCY AND FORGIVENESS ARE BOUNDLESS FOR THOSE WHO SEEK THEM SINCERELY.
6. **SHARE YOUR PLANS:** WRITE DOWN YOUR PLANS FOR YOUR FUTURE. DREAM BIG, AND DON'T BE AFRAID TO ASK FOR HIS BLESSINGS.
7. **CLOSE WITH HOPE AND FAITH:** END THE LETTER WITH HOPE AND FAITH IN GOD'S GRACE AND GUIDANCE. TRUST IN THE POWER OF PRAYER AND BELIEVE THAT YOUR WORDS WILL BE HEARD AND ANSWERED.

WHAT TO DO WITH THE LETTER?

YOU MAY CHOOSE TO KEEP THE LETTER IN A SPECIAL BOX, JOURNAL, OR MEMORY BOOK WHERE YOU CAN REVISIT IT WHENEVER YOU NEED COMFORT OR INSPIRATION. IF YOU FEEL COMFORTABLE, YOU COULD SHARE THE LETTER WITH A RELIGIOUS OR SPIRITUAL LEADER FOR GUIDANCE OR REFLECTION. YOU MAY WANT TO INCORPORATE THE LETTER INTO YOUR PRAYERS OR MEDITATION AS A WAY TO REAFFIRM YOUR GRATITUDE AND LOVE FOR GOD. KEEPING THE LETTER AS A REMINDER OF YOUR FAITH AND CONNECTION TO GOD CAN BE A COMFORTING AND UPLIFTING PRACTICE. INSPIRE SOMEONE TO DO THE SAME. THE DECISION OF WHAT TO DO WITH THE LETTER IS PERSONAL AND SHOULD BE BASED ON WHAT FEELS MEANINGFUL TO YOU.

"
GO, EAT YOUR FOOD WITH GLADNESS, AND DRINK YOUR WINE WITH A JOYFUL HEART, FOR GOD HAS ALREADY APPROVED WHAT YOU DO
ECCLESIASTES 9:7

"Go, eat your food with gladness, and drink your wine with a joyful heart, for God has already approved what you do."

Often, people work so hard chasing their dreams, that they forget to slow down and enjoy things that they already have. I am one of those people.

Proverbs 12:24-27 **"Hard work will give you power; being lazy will make you a slave."**

Another opposite side of people who like to be lazy and often like to say, "I could care less" or "I don't care." In Wikipedia, you can find the meaning of the word sloth - the word "sloth" is a translation of the Latin term acedia, which means "without care." mentally, acedia has a number of distinctive components, of which the most important is affectlessness, a lack of any feeling about self or others, a mind state that gives rise to boredom, rancor, apathy, and a passive, inert, or sluggish mentality.

Physically, acedia is fundamentally a cessation of motion and an indifference to work. Sloth can also be referred to as laziness. Two commentators consider the most accurate translation of acedia to be "self-pity," for it "conveys both the melancholy of the condition and self-centeredness upon which it is founded."

How do you Biblically overcome sloth? Ask God to help you. Focus on one task at a time, and remain yoked to the work God has given you to do every day.

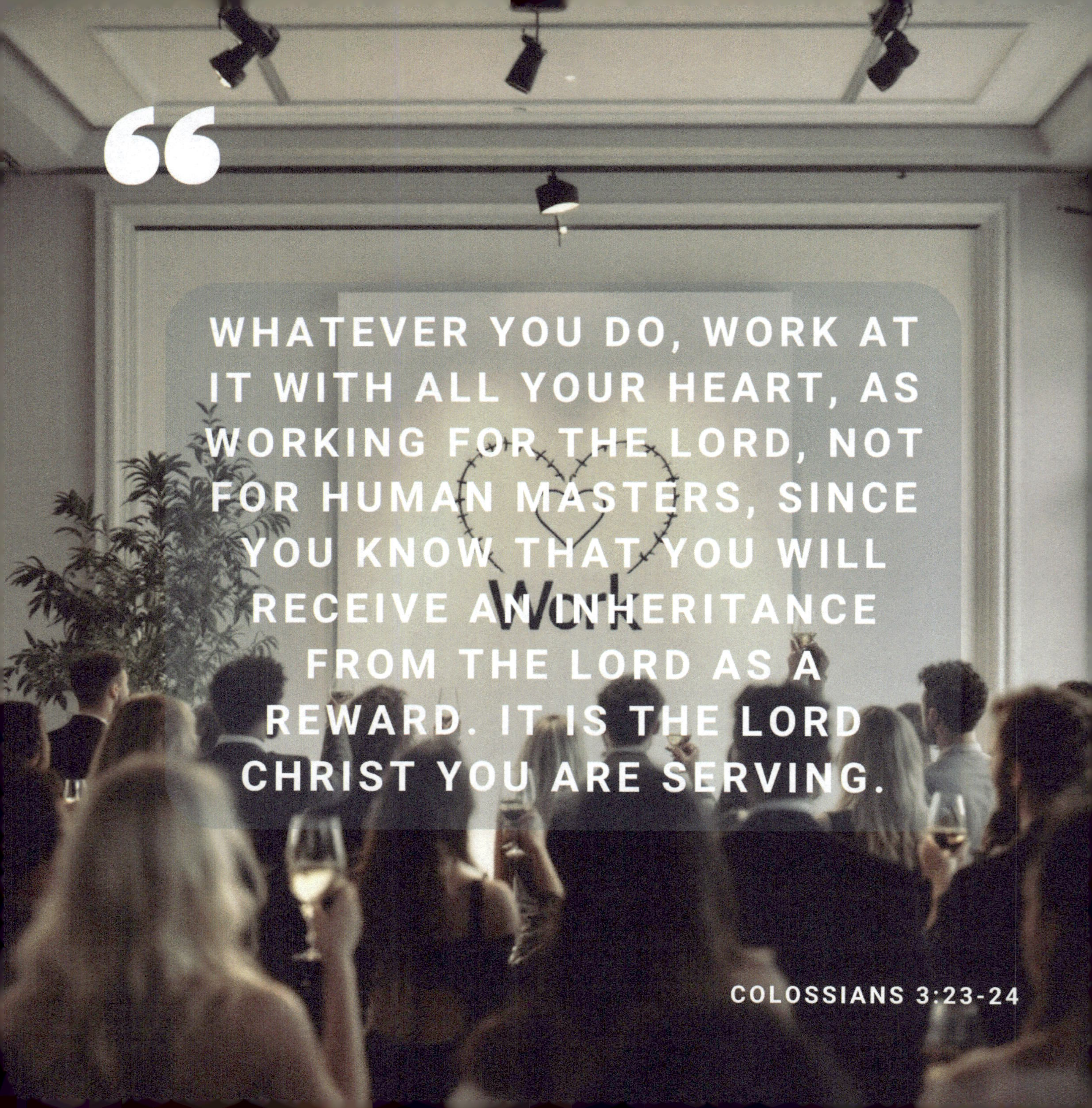
"
WHATEVER YOU DO, WORK AT IT WITH ALL YOUR HEART, AS WORKING FOR THE LORD, NOT FOR HUMAN MASTERS, SINCE YOU KNOW THAT YOU WILL RECEIVE AN INHERITANCE FROM THE LORD AS A REWARD. IT IS THE LORD CHRIST YOU ARE SERVING.
COLOSSIANS 3:23-24
Work

Do a daily examination and ask yourself: what was accomplished by the end of the day? Strive to get better every single day till it becomes a habit to be productive. I love those productive days; it gives me even more motivation and satisfaction. Part of it is based on my personal beliefs that I've learned from God's word.

We can pray, hope, have faith, and dream about our future, but remember, we also have to work as well, because faith alone without works is dead. James tells us:

James 2:14-17: "Don't question why you lack something, but question if you work for it."

Proverbs 6:9-11: "How long will you lie there, you sluggard? When will you get up from your sleep? A little sleep, a little slumber, a little folding of the hands to rest—and poverty will come on you like a thief and scarcity like an armed force."

It is very important to prioritize and organize schedules so we can enjoy people and things that already were given to us by God.

He reminds us that this life is too short, and His will is that we should enjoy the pleasures He has given us right now, so have a glass of wine with a joyful heart.

Julia

SALMON SOUP

THIS RECIPE IS A BIT OF A FAMILY SECRET. I FOUND IT TUCKED AWAY IN A STASH OF OLD LETTERS, AND I CAN ONLY IMAGINE THE JOY THIS HAS BROUGHT TO PREVIOUS GENERATIONS.

YOU WILL NEED:

- 1 ONION
- 1.75 LBS (800 G) FIRM POTATOES
- 4 CARROTS
- A PIECE OF THE WHITE PART OF A LEEK (ABOUT 3.5 OZ / 100 G)
- 1 FENNEL BULB
- 2 TABLESPOONS BUTTER
- 6 ⅓ CUPS (1.5 LITERS) WATER
- 3 DRIED BAY LEAVES
- 3.5 OZ (100 G) BROWNED BUTTER
- 1 LEMON
- ⅘ CUP (200 ML) HEAVY CREAM
- 1–1 ½ TEASPOONS FINE SEA SALT
- 1.5 LBS (700 G) SKINLESS, BONELESS SALMON FILLET

AS AN OLD-FASHIONED RECIPE, THERE IS A LOT OF BUTTER AND CREAM INCLUDED. IF YOU WANT, YOU CAN ALWAYS OMIT THE BUTTER AND LEAVE OUT THE CREAM FOR A CLEAR SOUP - THAT WORKS TOO, BUT ONCE IN A WHILE A HEAVY-DUTY SOUP IS IN ORDER.

PEEL AND DICE THE ONION, POTATOES, AND CARROTS. THINLY SLICE THE LEEK (WHITE PART ONLY) AND FENNEL.

HEAT 2 TABLESPOONS OF BUTTER IN A LARGE SOUP POT OVER MEDIUM HEAT. ADD THE ONION, LEEK, AND FENNEL. SAUTÉ UNTIL SOFTENED AND FRAGRANT, ABOUT 5–7 MINUTES.

ADD THE POTATOES, CARROTS, WATER, AND BAY LEAVES TO THE POT. BRING TO A BOIL, THEN REDUCE TO A SIMMER. COVER AND COOK FOR 15–20 MINUTES OR UNTIL THE VEGETABLES ARE TENDER.

WHILE THE VEGETABLES ARE SIMMERING, ZEST AND JUICE THE LEMON. CUT THE FISH FILLET INTO BITE-SIZED PIECES.

ONCE THE VEGETABLES ARE TENDER, REMOVE THE BAY LEAVES. STIR IN THE BROWNED BUTTER (3.5 OZ / 100 G), HEAVY CREAM, AND SEA SALT.

GENTLY ADD THE FISH PIECES TO THE SOUP. LET THEM COOK IN THE SIMMERING LIQUID FOR 5–7 MINUTES OR UNTIL THE FISH IS OPAQUE AND FLAKES EASILY WITH A FORK.

TASTE THE SOUP AND ADJUST THE SALT AND CREAM AS NEEDED.

LADLE THE SOUP INTO BOWLS AND GARNISH WITH FRESH DILL OR PARSLEY, LEMON ZEST, LEMON JUICE, IF DESIRED. SERVE WITH CRUSTY BREAD FOR A SATISFYING MEAL.

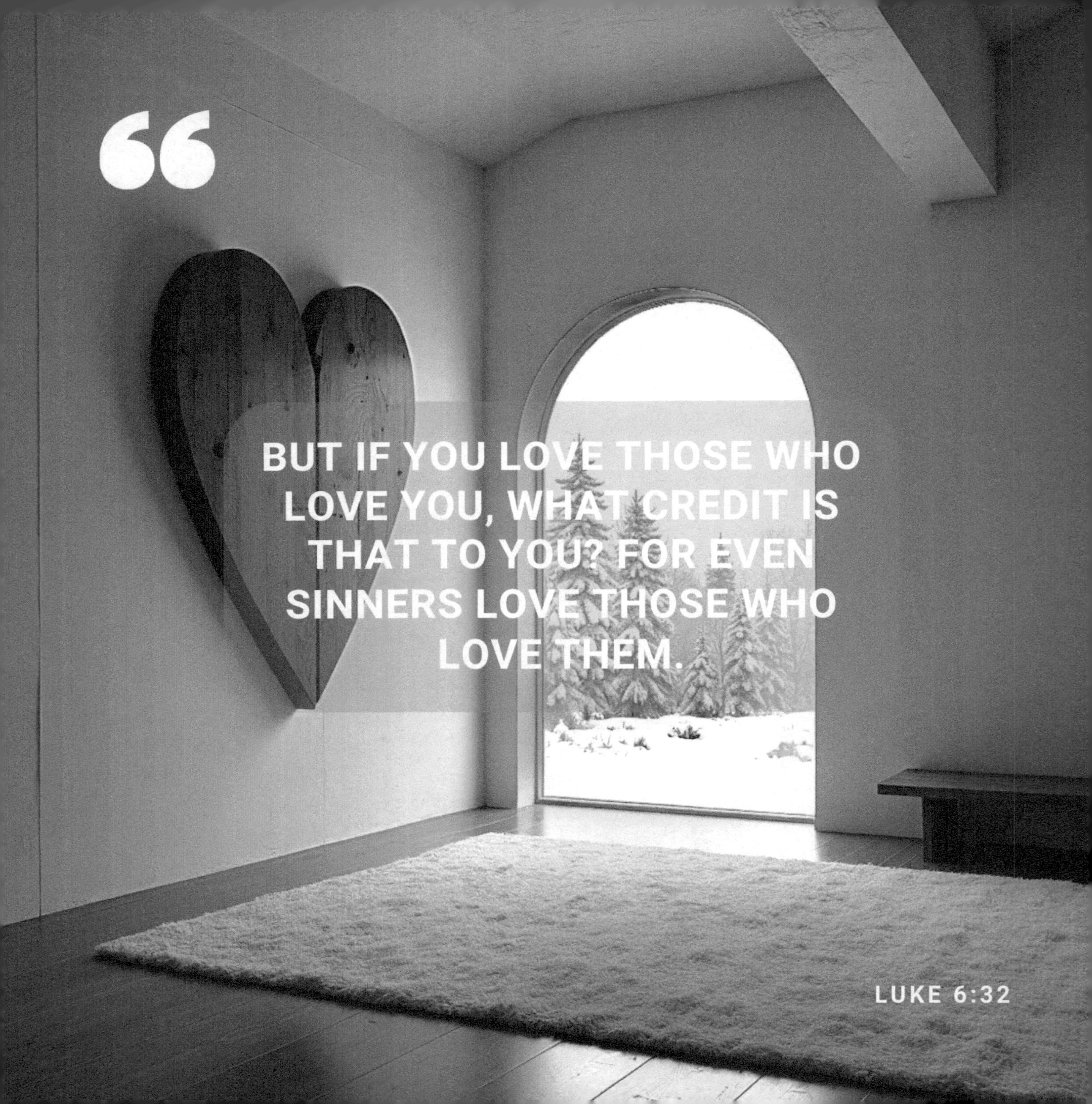
“
BUT IF YOU LOVE THOSE WHO LOVE YOU, WHAT CREDIT IS THAT TO YOU? FOR EVEN SINNERS LOVE THOSE WHO LOVE THEM.
LUKE 6:32

"But if you love those who love you, what credit is that to you? For even sinners love those who love them."

Well, you read that Bible verse. I'm not sure if I know you or perhaps you are a stranger, but I assure you that I love you. Now let me be honest, it won't be the kind of love like the one I feel towards my family or even my dog, but I know that I will do my best to love you because my Father told me so. It's extremely hard sometimes, especially to love those who brought you pain in the past or even in the present moment. It might be so difficult that you'll feel suffocated by the thought of it, but that is exactly where you can test your personal strength and wisdom that comes from God Himself. Of all the scriptures and Bible verses He provided for us through the Bible, He commands the two most important things.

Number one:

"You shall love the Lord your God with all your heart and with all your soul and with all your mind."

And number two:

"You shall love your neighbor as yourself."
(Matthew 22:37–40)

These two commandments are so critical that if you don't follow them, you can ruin your own future. By future, I mean your entire eternity - the endless existence. Think about it. Love you!

Julia

UKRAINIAN CABBAGE ROLLS (HOLUBTSI)

INGREDIENTS:

- 1 LARGE HEAD OF CABBAGE
- 1 LB GROUND PORK
- 1 LB GROUND BEEF
- 1 ONION, FINELY CHOPPED
- 1 CUP COOKED RICE
- 1 CAN OF TOMATO SAUCE
- BUTTER
- 1 TSP PAPRIKA
- SALT AND PEPPER TO TASTE
- 2 CUPS OF BEEF BROTH
- 2 BAY LEAVES
- SOUR CREAM FOR SERVING

DIRECTIONS:

1. CAREFULLY REMOVE THE OUTER LEAVES OF THE CABBAGE AND BOIL THE WHOLE HEAD IN A POT OF WATER FOR ABOUT 5-7 MINUTES UNTIL THE LEAVES ARE SOFT. REMOVE FROM WATER AND LET COOL.
2. IN A LARGE BOWL, MIX TOGETHER THE GROUND PORK, GROUND BEEF, ONION, COOKED RICE, GARLIC, PAPRIKA, SALT, AND PEPPER UNTIL WELL COMBINED.
3. GENTLY PEEL OFF CABBAGE LEAVES AND CUT OUT THE THICK STEM FROM EACH LEAF.
4. TAKE A CABBAGE LEAF AND PLACE A SPOONFUL OF THE MEAT MIXTURE IN THE CENTER. FOLD IN THE SIDES AND ROLL IT UP TO FORM A CABBAGE ROLL. REPEAT WITH THE REMAINING LEAVES AND FILLING.
5. IN A LARGE POT, ADD A LAYER OF CABBAGE LEAVES AT THE BOTTOM. PLACE THE CABBAGE ROLLS ON TOP, SEAM SIDE DOWN.
6. IN A SEPARATE BOWL, MIX TOGETHER THE TOMATO SAUCE, DICED TOMATOES, AND BEEF BROTH. POUR THIS MIXTURE OVER THE CABBAGE ROLLS.
7. COVER THE POT AND SIMMER OVER LOW HEAT FOR 1.5-2 HOURS OR UNTIL THE CABBAGE ROLLS ARE TENDER.
8. SERVE THE CABBAGE ROLLS HOT WITH A DOLLOP OF SOUR CREAM ON TOP. ENJOY YOUR TRADITIONAL UKRAINIAN MEAL!

SOMETIMES, PRAYERS MAY
NOT ALIGN WITH GOD’S WILL

This story is about a woman who lost more than half of her hearing when she was 3 years old. Her loved ones supported every surgery with hope for restoration. Growing up, she faced challenges and hurtful words, being labeled as "deaf," and enduring long stays in the hospital after surgeries. Because of it, she lost her best friend of 7 years after she told her, “We can’t be friends because you’re in the hospital too much.” Her world became even more silent and lonely.

Despite the hardships, there was a glimmer of hope in her life. At the age of 12, she discovered solace in the pages of a Children's Bible gifted to her by her Godmother. Through prayer, fasting, and devotion to her faith, she found peace in the midst of her silence.

As she was growing older, she began to realize the brutal reality that awaited her future. It was useless to pay for her Jurist education when she couldn’t hear lessons. Finding a job of her dreams seemed impossible, but she believed that one of those surgeries would restore her hearing, making her like everyone else.

She had such a strong faith and believed so strongly that she underwent lots of surgeries with prayers and hopes for restoration. After each operation, doctors said that as the scars healed, she would hear better. She paid attention to every sound she could catch, imagining that she was healed, but it didn't happen.

“
THREE TIMES, I PLEADED WITH THE LORD TO TAKE IT AWAY FROM ME. BUT HE SAID TO ME, “MY GRACE IS SUFFICIENT FOR YOU, FOR MY POWER IS MADE PERFECT IN WEAKNESS.” THEREFORE, I WILL BOAST ALL THE MORE GLADLY ABOUT MY WEAKNESSES SO THAT CHRIST’S POWER MAY REST ON ME.
2 CORINTHIANS 12:8-9

She did it again and again and again, a total of 14 surgeries. Each time, believing that the next one would restore her hearing. But as each surgery came and went, the silence remained unbroken. She would keep trying, but this time, her doctor said - it's impossible.

Left with a disability and questions for the Lord — why did this happen to her at the age of 3? Why couldn't she be healed as she begged for His mercy? She learned to appreciate the smallest sounds, cherishing them as gifts that were left in her Body and put her trust in Him.

IN 2 Corinthians 12:8, Paul pleaded Three times with the Lord to take away HIS THORN. "But he said to me, "My grace is sufficient for you, for my power is made perfect in weakness. Therefore, I will boast all the more gladly about my weaknesses, so that Christ's power may rest on me (2 Corinthians 12:9-10)". God's purpose was to keep Paul humble and dependent on God.

Today, she is grateful for all the trials and thankful for the latest technology that allows her to hear the world and music through her hearing aids in both ears. She believes that God blessed her with these challenges to reveal His strength. Perhaps He saved her soul by redirecting her focus towards Him instead of chasing after a career and money, despite her love for work. She found joy in creating videos, loves photography where she can "hear" through her eyes, and she never lost her faith. She knows that God has a bigger plan for her future. She is me.

Julia

…WHEN ITS BRANCH HAS ALREADY BECOME TENDER AND PUTS FORTH LEAVES, YOU KNOW THAT SUMMER IS NEAR. SO YOU ALSO, WHEN YOU SEE ALL THESE THINGS, KNOW THAT IT IS NEAR—AT THE DOORS!
JESUS

How can we feel content when we hear questions like these: "Are you ready and looking for the Second Coming of Jesus Christ?" "What will be the sign of His coming and of the end of the age?"

Jesus spoke in parables. The word "parable" is Greek. It means to "lay alongside." So Jesus used an earthly story and laid it alongside a spiritual reality for us to learn and deeply understand the meaning behind His teachings. "Learn" means to "genuinely understand." It was used by Paul in Philippians 4:11: "I have learned in whatever state I am, to be content." This is the answer to the questions above - learn.

In Matthew 24:32-34 Jesus says: "Now learn this parable from the fig tree: When its branch has already become tender and puts forth leaves, you know that summer is near. So you also, when you see all these things, know that it is near—at the doors! Assuredly, I say to you, this generation will by no means pass away till all these things take place." *(see also Mark 13:28-31; Luke 21:29-33)*

One way to interpret this passage:

- Israel is the fig tree.
- The words, "When its branch has already become tender and puts forth leaves, you know that summer is near," refers to Israel becoming a nation in 1948.
- A generation is 70-80 years.
- Jesus said the generation that sees Israel become a nation will not pass away.

BUT OF THAT DAY AND HOUR, NO ONE KNOWS...

Jesus said, “When you see all these things, know that it is near—at the doors!” What things? Everything Jesus discussed in the previous verses:

- Mark 13:1-2 & Matthew 24:1-2 & Luke 21:5-6 – The destruction of the temple
- Mark 13:3-13 & Matthew 24:3-14 & Luke 21:7-19 – The signs of the times and the end of the age
- Luke 21:20-24 – The destruction of Jerusalem
- Numbers 19:1-2 & Daniel 9:24-27 - Rebuilding the Temple and the sacrifice of the red heifer.
- Mark 13:14-23 & Matthew 24:15-28 – The Great Tribulation
- Mark 13:24-27 & Matthew 24:29-31 & Luke 21:25-28 – Jesus’ Second Coming

There are a lot of different ways to interpret what Jesus said, “But of that day and hour no one knows, not even the angels of heaven, but My Father only,” Jesus said. How could Jesus be God and not know when He is coming back? Philippians 2:6 says, "Who, though He was in the form of God, did not consider equality with God something to be grasped.” It illustrates the humility of Jesus, who was God but did not claim His rights as God while he was on Earth.

In Matthew 16:28, Jesus said: “Truly I say unto you, there are some standing here, who may not taste of death, until they may see the Son of man coming in His kingdom." Hebrews 9:28 - so Christ, having been offered once to bear the sins of many, will appear a second time, not to deal with sin, but to save those who are eagerly waiting for him.

Seeing the days are at hand, may the warnings of Christ prompt us to truly examine ourselves.

The time for the faithful to look up and rejoice! Julia

CHERRY RICOTTA CHEESECAKE

1 1/4 CUPS GRAHAM CRACKER CRUMBS

¼ CUP BUTTER, MELTED

2 TBS. + ¾ CUP SUGAR

2 IBS. RICOTTA CHEESE

4 EGGS

3 TBS. ALL-PURPOSE FLOUR

1 TSP. VANILLA EXTRACT

1 TSP. GRATED LEMON ZEST

1/8 TSP. SALT

1 CUP CHERRY PIE FILLING

DIRECTIONS:

HEAT OVEN TO 325°F.

GREASE A 9" SPRINGFORM PAN.

IN A BOWL, COMBINE CRUMBS, BUTTER AND

2 TBS. SUGAR: PRESS INTO THE BOTTOM OF THE PAN.

BAKE UNTIL SET, ABOUT 8 MIN.

LET COOL COMPLETELY.

ON MEDIUM SPEED, BEAT CHEESE AND ¾ CUP SUGAR UNTIL SMOOTH. BEAT IN EGGS ONE AT A TIME, THEN FLOUR, VANILLA, ZEST AND SALT.

POUR OVER CRUST.

BAKE UNTIL CENTER JIGGLES SLIGHTLY, 1 HR., 15 MIN.

RUN KNIFE AROUND SIDE OF CAKE; COOL ON RACK.

COVER; CHILL OVERNIGHT.

REMOVE THE SIDE OF PAN. TOP WITH FILLING

ENJOY!

"
MAY THE GOD OF HOPE FILL
YOU WITH ALL JOY AND PEACE
IN BELIEVING SO THAT BY THE
POWER OF THE HOLY SPIRIT,
YOU MAY ABOUND IN HOPE.
ROMANS 15:13

Oh, praise to the heavens, for we are all welcomed and accepted by our loving and gracious God! Let us bask in the glory of His infinite love, for in Acts 10:34-35, it is written,

"God plays no favorites, that God accepts every person whatever His or her culture or ethnic background, that God welcomes all who revere Him and do right."

Revere means to feel deep respect or admiration. Let the words of Romans 2:11 fill your soul with joy, "For God shows no partiality." it matters not where you come from, what you look like, or what you have; God's love knows no bounds. Rejoice in the knowledge that you are part of His family, embraced in His everlasting arms. What a beautiful truth to cling to!

No matter the trials we face or the challenges that come our way, let us hold fast to the promises of the Lord. His love is everlasting, His mercy is endless, and His grace is sufficient for all our needs. If we put our trust in Him, we will find true joy that surpasses all understanding.

In times of sorrow and uncertainty, let us turn to the words "FEAR NOT" mentioned 365 times in the Bible. 365 times, he repeated Himself for you not to be afraid! So FEAR NOT! With God by our side, we can face any challenge with courage and joy in our hearts.

In times of doubt and loneliness, remember that you belong to God. Psalm 139:14 reminds us that we are fearfully and wonderfully made by our Creator, with a purpose and a place in His divine plan. Do not be discouraged by worldly standards, for in God's eyes, you are cherished beyond measure.

MAY YOUR
HEART BE
FOREVER
JOYFUL,
KNOWING THAT
YOUR SPIRITUAL
JOURNEY
IS GUIDED BY
DIVINE LOVE
JOYFUL & SPIRITUAL

Again, let us rejoice, for today is a gift from God, filled with blessings and grace beyond measure. Let us open our hearts to His love, let it transform us from within, and let our souls sing praises to the heavens, for we are deeply loved by the Creator of all things. Philippians 4:4:

"Rejoice in the Lord always; again, I will say, rejoice."

Indeed, each moment is a divine opportunity to experience the joy and wonder of God's presence in our lives. Psalm 30:5 - "For His anger is but for a moment, and His favor is for a lifetime. Weeping may tarry for the night, but joy comes with the morning".

Take heart in the comfort that God's love is unconditional and unwavering. His blessings are abundant, and His presence is ever near. May our hearts overflow with gratitude and joy as we walk in faith and fellowship with our Heavenly Father.

Amen.

Julia

Writing this book has been an extraordinary joy and a profound privilege. It feels as though God Himself has guided us on this incredible journey. One thing we've discovered along the way is the truth of His promise: when we take the time to step into His presence, he faithfully draws near to us. This season of writing has been a roller coaster of emotions and experiences—filled with both exhilarating highs and challenging lows. Yet, through it all, God has been our constant companion, our unwavering source of peace and inspiration. Truly, He is our faithful friend.

We set out to create the kind of book we would have cherished as we prepared to face the cold and quiet of winter—a season that invites us to pause, reflect, and savor life's simple joys. Winter, with its stillness and beauty, offers a unique opportunity to reconnect with ourselves and with God. Within these pages, we've shared our best-kept secrets for not just surviving but flourishing during this season. Now, these treasures are yours to enjoy. We hope this book has been as much of a delight for you to read as it was for us to create.

Our dream is to inspire you to embrace the rhythms of each season with purpose and grace, knowing that every moment—no matter how cold or dark—can hold the seeds of renewal and hope.

Until we meet again in the spring, may your heart stay warm, your spirit light, and your journey bright.

with love and gratitude.
Julia & Sofia

MAY THE GOD OF HOPE FILL
YOU WITH ALL JOY AND PEACE
IN BELIEVING, SO THAT BY THE
POWER OF THE HOLY SPIRIT
YOU MAY ABOUND IN HOPE
ROMANS 15:13

JULIA RENO, A DYNAMIC UKRAINIAN-BORN WRITER AND CONTENT CREATOR, IS THE FORCE BEHIND @JULIARENO_OFFICIAL, WHERE SHE CAPTIVATES HER AUDIENCE WITH INSPIRING LIFESTYLE CONTENT AND MASTERFUL VISUAL STORYTELLING. A HARVARD-CERTIFIED ENTREPRENEUR, JULIA HAS A SHARP EYE FOR THE LATEST TRENDS IN FASHION, HOME DECOR, AND ENTERTAINMENT, BLENDING STYLE WITH SUBSTANCE. WITH AN UNWAVERING PASSION FOR GOD'S WORD, SHE STRIVES TO MAKE A MEANINGFUL IMPACT THAT EXTENDS FAR BEYOND THE DIGITAL WORLD, LEAVING A LASTING LEGACY. HER LIFE AND WORK ARE DEEPLY GROUNDED IN HER FAITH AS A DEVOTED FOLLOWER OF JESUS CHRIST, FUELING HER JOURNEY OF PERSONAL GROWTH WHILE UPLIFTING AND INSPIRING OTHERS ALONG THE WAY.

SOFIA KAUKO-VALLI IS A TRANSFORMATIVE POSITIVE PSYCHOLOGY PRACTITIONER AND THE VISIONARY VOICE BEHIND @DRSOFIAKAUKO_VALLI. WITH A MISSION TO EMPOWER OTHERS TO DISCOVER THEIR INNER HERO AND BUILD UNSHAKABLE RESILIENCE, SOFIA BLENDS HER EXPERTISE WITH A DEEP AND PERSONAL PASSION FOR GROWTH AND HEALING. GUIDED BY AN INTENSE LOVE FOR GOD'S PRESENCE, SHE DRAWS DAILY INSPIRATION FROM THE BEAUTY OF NATURE AND THE BOUNDLESS GOODNESS AND KINDNESS OF THE CREATOR. SOFIA'S WORK IS MORE THAN A PROFESSION—IT'S A CALLING TO HELP OTHERS LIVE BOLDLY, JOYFULLY, AND AUTHENTICALLY IN ALIGNMENT WITH THEIR IDENTITY IN CHRIST.

Made in the USA
Monee, IL
19 April 2025

16043063R00122